Gray Matter, Dark Matter, and Doesn't Matter

Gray Matter, Dark Matter, and Doesn't Matter

Essays on the Mind, the Universe, and Whatever

HARRY L. SERIO

RESOURCE *Publications* • Eugene, Oregon

GRAY MATTER, DARK MATTER, AND DOESN'T MATTER
Essays on the Mind, the Universe, and Whatever

Resource Publications
An Imprint of Wipf and Stock Publishers
199 W. 8th Ave., Suite 3
Eugene, OR 97401

www.wipfandstock.com

PAPERBACK ISBN: 979-8-3852-2345-9
HARDCOVER ISBN: 979-8-3852-2346-6
EBOOK ISBN: 979-8-3852-2347-3

06/20/24

Contents

Preface	vii
Act of Creation	1
Galaxies Far, Far Away	3
Speculation	7
What Do We Know?	9
Dark Matter	11
Little Things Mean a Lot	14
Mind Your Own Business	17
"One Hand Clapping"	20
The Psi Factor	23
The Paranormal and the Church	28
"Becoming a Ghost"	34
"Will Ye No Come Back Again?"	38
The Blob	41
Apparition with a Mission	44
Naming the Devil	48
Ophidiophobia	51
Not in the Stars But in Ourselves	53
Monkey on Fire	57
Lost Horizons	60
When You Pray	64
Psychoanalyzing God	67
Kirkridge	72

Contents

Pilger Ruh   76
"A Feather on the Breath of God"   80
Visions of St. Joan   83
Knowing Snow   86
Failure to Communicate   90
Ars Gratia Artis   93
Creating the Architecture of a Spiritual Path   101
"Tell Me Your Name"   108
Homework   112
Uncle Peppers   116
Cattitudes   119
The Voice of Many Angels   122
The Golden Lamp   125
Church Building Abandoned   129
To Know the Place Where You Belong   131
Bibliography   135

PREFACE

What are the limits of human cognition? How do we know anything? Who we are, what we do, who we interact with, where we live, what we read, what we watch on television, indeed our exposure to the world around us affects how we think and how we make sense of our environment. The world is inside of our brains. Our gray matter contains all of our memories and enables the past to affect our future. What we remember shapes who we are.

Scientists are investigating the dark matter of the universe which supposedly comprises 85 percent of all that is. When Carl Jung posed the idea of a collective unconscious, I am not so sure that it is limited to the aggregation of human minds. When we speak of God, how do we define what or who God is? God may very well be a universal consciousness that pervades all that is. Our individual experiences may be part of a universal whole affecting the entirety of creation.

The title of this book includes the words "Doesn't Matter," but in a sense, everything matters. Everything that appears insignificant, irrelevant, and doesn't matter has an effect upon the universe, and we may not know what it is until the eschaton, the final conclusion of all that is, if indeed there will be an end. Or just another beginning.

This book contains a series of essays that have some relevance to my own life and to my relationship with others. Some may not matter to the reader, but all relate to some aspect of our mutual existence.

PREFACE

I encourage you to explore your own life, your own memories, the stories that help to make you who you are, so that you may discover your own reason for being and your own place in the universe.

ACT OF CREATION

In the first story of creation in Genesis, the Bible says, "In the beginning when God created the heavens and the earth" (Gen 1:1). One must assume that "the heavens" are everything extraterrestrial or the entire universe. The Spirit of God moved through the darkness, and God said, "Let there be light" (Gen 1:3). If God actually said it, then light was not the first act of creation. It was sound. Maybe to be more accurate, the Bible should have said that God first created the electromagnetic spectrum.

However, both light and sound need a medium in which to travel. Perhaps the origin of the universe was not a "Big Bang" but rather an "Explosive Silence."

The human mind is not able to comprehend the vastness of the universe. A photographic image of just one part of the heavens shows billions and billions of points of light, each representing a galaxy. Each galaxy contains billions of stars, with each star containing innumerable planets. Is there a number large enough to gauge the possibility of life forms throughout the universe?

In the same way, can the human mind fully grasp the meaning of God? When an atheist tells me that there is no such thing as God, my first statement to him is, "Explain yourself!" How do we explain creation, the very idea of existence, or intelligent design? Science has many answers that go back to the infinitesimal particles that comprise matter, even to recognize that the end result of this reduction is vibration—sound. But from where did the design emanate? What is the reasoning behind the process of evolution?

1

Gray Matter, Dark Matter, and Doesn't Matter

Evolution is the process of trial and error. A species that survives will eventually prevail and continue. Does the same process also apply to the question of good and evil? Are we to assume that good will eventually prevail over evil? This is the question of theodicy that theologians wrestle with. If an omniscient and omnipotent God is good, why does this God permit evil to exist? Or is it that God no longer cares about his creation or is powerless to eliminate evil? This branch of theology is so extensive, consisting of various definitions of what is good and what is evil, and ultimately, who and what "God" is. I prefer Yogi Berra's advice: "It ain't over till it's over." In the meantime, I will proceed through this life in a walk of faith.

The poet James Russell Lowell opposed the Mexican-American War and in 1845 wrote the poem "The Present Crisis," which was later used by William Lloyd Garrison and other abolitionists in the antislavery movement. In the conflict between Truth and Wrong "behind the dim unknown / Standeth God within the shadow, keeping watch above his own."[1]

The universe is a process that inevitably moves to a conclusion (and perhaps to start over again). The God of creation exists within each person and in all that is. There is intentionality to the universe, and as the Scriptures often say, that which is hidden will be revealed. In the eschaton, we shall know, and as our faith maintains, love will prevail.

1. Lowell, "Present Crisis."

GALAXIES FAR, FAR AWAY

When I was six years old I could name all the planets and their satellites. I didn't think much of this at the time, but it so impressed my relatives that they predicted I would become an astronomer.

I did make many visits to the Hayden Planetarium in New York and the Newark Museum Planetarium and was mesmerized by the ethereal voice speaking about the planets and the galaxies far, far away. I would rush home from school to turn on the television and watch *Flash Gordon*; *Buck Rogers*; *Tom Corbett, Space Cadet* (no, not the Pennsylvania governor); and all the other space shows and movies.

My first-grade teacher gave the class an assignment to write an essay about how we would like to spend our summer vacation. I said, "on Mars," but I would have to wait since they weren't scheduling any flights soon.

What interested me about the universe was its vastness beyond comprehension. The circularity of the galaxy was perplexing to my pre-Newtonian mind. Since my small hands were prone to dropping things, I had a rudimentary understanding of gravity, but when applied to the universe, it was so overwhelming. Some astro-philosophers and theoreticians were saying that if you could fly into infinity, you would end up returning to where you started. Perhaps the poet T. S. Eliot was on to something when he said that the end of all our exploring "will be to arrive where we started and know the place for the first time."[2]

The contemplation of the universe led me to philosophical speculation about its origin. Sunday School answers just didn't satisfy. That God did it wasn't enough. I wanted to know why. One of my Sunday School teachers, who happened to be the minister's wife, said that God created the universe so that we could testify to the existence of God. Since an artist is known by what she creates, so we give meaning to the existence of the creator—kind of like, "I think, therefore God is."

My uncle told me that I think too much and asked too many questions. He told me to just enjoy life and be grateful that I am alive. Maybe that was an early attempt at the expression of enjoying the journey and not worrying about the destination. But I have always wanted to know where I was going and "What's it all about, Alfie?" My uncle may have been right—the journey is the destination.

The exploration of the universe was to go where no one had gone before. My childhood friends would talk about UFOs, and some believed they actually saw one. When I was pastor in the small village of Martins Creeks, Pennsylvania, one of my church members, who was the police chief in the town, claimed that he had spotted a UFO and chased the low-flying craft on Little Creek Road. The question always seemed to be whether there was intelligent life elsewhere in the universe. Bill Watterson of *Calvin and Hobbes* once said, "The surest sign that intelligent life exists elsewhere in the universe is that it has never tried to contact us."[3] One of my college professors said that the pilots of the UFOs couldn't be that smart if they traveled thousands of miles through the universe only to flash a few lights in our skies.

All of the science fiction stories, books, and movies that I have read or seen were predicated on human reasoning and logic. Is it possible that there might be other ways of thinking? Of course,

2. Eliot, "We Shall Not Cease . . ."
3. Watterson, "The Surest Sign . . ."

we wouldn't know that since we are limited by our own human cognition.

It may very well be that there is intelligent life throughout the universe and that these alien life forms have tried to contact us, but we just don't understand the language. I once had the privilege of meeting Carl Sagan at a conference for United Church of Christ ministers in Florida. It was shortly after his *Cosmos* series aired on PBS, and he was talking about the fifteen billion years of cosmic evolution that have transformed matter into life and consciousness. He made a point that has fascinated me ever since. We consist of the dust of stars, the atoms of our bodies having their origins in galaxies far, far away.

A simple observation: Look at the vein in the back of your hand. What makes it red?

Hemoglobin. What makes hemoglobin? Iron. Where do we get iron? Only from the stars. And if a mineral is heavier than iron, it's been made in a supernova. In other words, we do not have an atom in our bodies that isn't the product of some dead star.

Carl Sagan was indeed an astral archaeologist who took us back to the beginnings of the universe in the search for our own origin. He was not the first to declare that we are made of dust. God made us from the "dust of the ground," says Genesis (2:7), but it must have been stardust, the swirling stuff of exploding gas and dust that is flung into interstellar space as a dying star's core collapses.

Neil DeGrasse Tyson, astrophysicist and director of the Hayden Planetarium, puts it this way: "The atoms of our bodies are traceable to stars that manufactured them in their cores and exploded these enriched ingredients across our galaxy, billions of years ago. For this reason, we are biologically connected to every other living thing in the world. We are chemically connected to all molecules on Earth. And we are atomically connected to all atoms in the universe. We are not figuratively, but literally stardust."[4]

If humans are made of stardust, can it not also be possible that other life in the universe may also have been derived from the

4. Tyson, "Atoms of Our Bodies . . ."

dust of exploding stars? Erich von Daniken and other writers have expressed the fantastic idea that Earth has been visited by ancient astronauts. Some have even posited these aliens as an explanation for what we have difficulty comprehending, such as how the pyramids of Egypt or Stonehenge of Salisbury Plain were constructed. The use of extraterrestrials as an answer to what we have yet to learn may seem as far-fetched as the possibility that humans were once extraterrestrials.

Francis Crick once suggested that life on Earth originated elsewhere in the universe and was transported here by alien life forms, the so-called panspermia theory.[5] Perhaps the reported Unidentified Aerial Phenomena (the Air Force has replaced UFOs with UAPs) are the ETs checking on our progress in the same way that gardeners tend their gardens. Still, other scientists speculate that the seeds of life may have come from microscopic spores transported by a comet.[6]

As difficult as it might be that we could understand what aliens may be trying to communicate to us, it is also hard to comprehend that somewhere in some distant galaxy an alien will make sense of the message and diagrams sent by Pioneer 10 and Voyager space probes from NASA's Search for Extraterrestrial Intelligence (SETI) program.

The biggest mystery for science is the question of how it all began. Where did the idea and the design for existence come from? The answer will not come from space probes or spectro-analysis or even extraterrestrials, but only from faith in a creator God, and even then the mystery remains.

---

5. Casti, *Paradigms Lost*, 115–118.
6. Casti, *Paradigms Lost*, 119.

SPECULATION

Francis Crick and Carl Sagan both speculate that the seeds of life on Earth may have emanated from elsewhere in the universe and were brought here by extraterrestrials (ETs). This certainly makes sense. There are some ten billion habitable worlds in our galaxy alone, so the odds are that we are not alone. And with billions of years to develop intelligence and technology, it makes sense that there might be an advanced form of life existing beyond the Earth.

The SETI program has been sending radio transmissions into outer space since the 1980s, but the ETs seem to just hang up on us. Stephen Hawking said that we might just be inviting an invasion.

However, would ETs think like us? Would our system of logical cognition communicate? What language would ETs use that we might understand?

In medieval times angels were considered extraterrestrials, residents of heaven who sometimes made earthly appearances in order to convey messages from God. The apostle Paul had said that love was the key to understanding the tongues of angels (1 Cor 13:1). In an effort to understand the native language of angels, one attempt was made by having newborn babies raised without hearing the spoken language of those caring for them, so that as they matured, they might speak in the forgotten language of angels.

It's a philosophical and theological question. When we pray, when we talk to God, who is listening? When God speaks to us, how do we interpret God's language? "For my thoughts are not your thoughts, nor are your ways my ways, says the Lord" (Isa 55:8). Are we just talking to ourselves?

Thousands of books by scientists and theologians seek to explain how life, consciousness, and thought came into being. But the greater question is where did the design originate? We may be able to explain the "how" of creation, but the "why" of existence eludes us. And so we rely on myth and religion.

Years ago I had been visiting a member of my congregation who had lived a very full life, traveled much, raised a large family, and received several service awards for his work in the community. He had just celebrated his ninety-fourth birthday, and his granddaughter called me to say that he was dying. When I came to his home, he was lying in his bed but very much alert and wanting to talk about all of the significant experiences he had had and his impending departure from this life. He asked, "Is that all there is? What was that all about?" He was asking the "why" question.

I could not explain the reason for his ninety-four years on this earth, except with the old adage that it was the journey itself that mattered. Who he was, what he had learned from his rich experiences, what he gave to others, what he had meant to his many friends and family, more than fulfilled his purpose for living. The Bible may be right when it says that in the end all things will be revealed and that there really is no end, just another beginning.

WHAT DO WE KNOW?

A continuing philosophical question is not only what we know but how we know it—and more importantly, what it means "to know."

Often in helping persons through the final stage of this segment of existence, I occasionally hear the fear expressed about what comes after death: "What if there is nothing there? What if all reality is a product of the brain's delusion? What if death is oblivion?"

The temptation is to respond with, "Well, then you will have nothing to worry about."

Theories of knowing are called into question as the reality of a creating intelligence comes under attack by some neo-Darwinians who see no use for a deity to explain creation. Richard Dawkins, Daniel Dennett, Sam Harris, and others offer their brand of weird science to postulate the non-existence of God. Dawkins has created his own fishbowl of science and stated that this is all there is. He cannot think outside the box of scientific imperialism.

In the fifteenth century, a stone marker stood at the Pillars of Hercules with the words, "*Ne Plus Ultra*"—"Nothing More Beyond." After Columbus' voyages, Spanish *real* coins bore the inscription "*Plus Ultra*." As soon as we establish limits there will always be someone to push beyond it.

While Dawkins mounts a vicious attack against religion, some of it justifiable, he also condemns the worship of mystery and the unscientific probing of the paranormal. Anecdotal evidence is not acceptable to him. Mediumship, near-death recollections, rein-carnation, and other "pseudo-apprehensions" of alternate realities would be described not as paranormal but paranoia—mind beside itself or outside the scientific box. He rejects the "God of the gaps" strategy, which theologian Dietrich Bonhoeffer also condemned. This strategy relegates to God all that we do not understand and says that as our knowledge increases, our need for God decreases. He falsely assumes that mystics "exult in mystery and want it to stay mysterious," and "that it is a virtue to be satisfied with not understanding."[1]

Mystics appreciate mystery but do not worship it. They seek instead to transcend it, to search for the ultimate understanding of the meaning and purpose of existence. To frame the nature and reality of God as an unprovable hypothesis is not part of the mystic's equation. To Dawkins, mysticism may be "paranoia," but to those who have had the experience it is more like "exo-noia," being out of one's mind in the sense that so much of existence cannot be processed by the brain-mind mechanism.

Richard Dawkins coined the term "meme" in his 1976 book *The Selfish Gene*. Memes are to culture as genes are to biology. They are packages of thought, racial memories, etc., that are passed along with genetic material from generation to generation. We might speculate that this memetic material might exist outside of its carrier and that this is what is perceived by psychics, mediums, visionaries, and mystics and compare it to the Sanskrit Akashic records, or Jung's collective unconscious, or discarnate residual energy. But we can talk about that at another time.

1. Dawkins, *God Delusion*, 125–126.

DARK MATTER

How did it all begin?
There was a time in my life, during my years in elementary school, when I had an interest in astronomy. I would read any book I could find on the galaxies, what they had to say about the planets in our solar system, and whether life could exist on any of them. I kept hoping that somebody from Mars would visit us, so I could ask the many questions that I had.

I remember when in eighth grade I was fumbling around in my desk looking for a book that I had brought to school and my teacher, Mr. Dacey, asked, "What's the matter?" I replied somewhat pedantically, "Matter is anything having weight and occupying space." This was many years before the rediscovery of dark matter which has no weight and may not occupy any space yet exerts a gravitational pull.

My childhood research eventually evolved into a wider cosmology. My universe was expanding, and I wanted to know how it all began. Human minds cannot fully fathom the vastness of the universe and all that it might contain. Scientists in recent decades have come up with the idea of "dark matter" to represent an invisible force in the universe that interacts with galaxies, the many systems of stars that exist in the observable and unobservable heavens. This dark matter possesses gravitational force, but modern science can't seem to find it. Since it doesn't reflect or emit light or interact in any way with the electromagnetic spectrum, the only evidence of its existence is its effect on other forms of matter. And yet scientists believe that dark matter (and dark energy) constitute 95% of the known universe. There is too much that we don't know.

I am reminded of Alexander Pope's "Essay on Criticism" when he says:

> A little learning is a dangerous thing;
> Drink deep, or taste not the Pierian spring:
> There shallow draughts intoxicate the brain,
> And drinking largely sobers us again.[1]

The Pierian Spring was located near Mount Olympus, the home of the ancient Greek gods, and was regarded as the source of all knowledge that the muses dispersed. I understand it to mean in our time that we don't know all there is to know and that we cannot probe the mind of God to explain the nature of creation. The small sips of knowledge are enough to confuse rather than enlighten, but when we drink enough, we know that we don't know. Those who are truly wise are aware of their limitations.

How do we justify our own existence? From where did the idea of existence itself derive? Why are things the way they are? Evolution as a process is not a complete answer since the process itself needed to be conceived by some intelligence. We often use the term "God" to represent all that we do not understand, all the dark matter of the universe.

The Bible tells us that we are created in the image of God. It may also be that God is created in the image of humans. The spirit of God that invented humans is part of each person that has ever lived and furthermore in all living and inanimate things in the universe. The concept of panentheism affirms that the presence of God is in all things, in the very atoms and subatomic particles. When these particles—baryons, muons, leptons, etc.—are further reduced, there is nothing there but energy—or spirit.

Johannes Kepler, the German astronomer and mathematician, once said, "I think Thy thoughts after Thee, O God."[2] These words are engraved on the wall of the Pfahler Science Building at

1. Pope, "Essay on Criticism."
2. Dao, "Man of Science."

my alma mater, Ursinus College. We may think God's thoughts after God, but often there is something lost in translation. And so God needed to remind the Jews,

> For my thoughts are not your thoughts,
> nor are your ways my ways, says the Lord.
> For as the heavens are higher than the earth,
> so are my ways higher than your ways
> and my thoughts than your thoughts. (Isa 55:8–9)

God's thoughts come to us in many ways: through our own cognitive abilities, through inspiration and contemplation, through our discernment of the events of our times, and also through the dark speech of dreams and visions. God bids us to be still and know that God is God (Ps 46:10). We cannot grasp the fullness of God through our own intellect, or our own understanding. Ultimately, we walk by faith and not by sight, trusting where we cannot see.

The one element that science has not entered into its equations in its attempt to explain dark matter and the origin of the universe is love. What we call God is simply love in its purest form, God's desire to be at one with all that God has created, and the desire that all of God's creation be at one with God. Anything else doesn't matter.

LITTLE THINGS MEAN A LOT

According to the Old Testament book of Genesis, sound and light are the first creations of that which called the world into being and conceived the design of life and the universe. "And God said (sound), let there be light." It may very well be that the electromagnetic spectrum preceded all other matter. Light consists of photons which scientists say are massless but move in waves. Sound, which is also part of the spectrum, like light, consists of phonons that are also particles in motion. Sound, light, and matter, when reduced to their basic subatomic structure, are vibrational. There is nothing there. Thus, reality may be illusional.

The universe is comprised of an infinite number of atoms. It is all small stuff that makes up the whole. This is also true of life, which is the aggregation of both small and large events. So many of the events in our lives are so small that we deem them insignificant, but they can affect our lives for years to come, often in life-altering ways.

Benjamin Franklin, perhaps remembering Shakespeare's *Richard III*, who at Bosworth Field cried "My kingdom for a horse," wrote:

> For want of a nail the shoe was lost. For want of a shoe the horse was lost. For want of a horse the rider was lost. For want of a rider the battle was lost. And all for the want of a horseshoe-nail.[1]

1. Franklin, "For Want of a Nail . . ."

When I was in my early teens, my church denomination ran an annual essay and art contest on the theme of stewardship. My home church, St. Stephan's Evangelical and Reformed Church in Newark, New Jersey, offered as first prize a one-week vacation at a church camp in Pennsylvania. My mother wrote the essay for me, but when I looked at it, I said, "I can do better than that" and revised the document before submitting it. I won the local contest and the pastor drove me and two others to Camp Fernbrook near Pottstown. That turned out to be a life-changing event. I was to return to Fernbrook and later Camp Mensch Mill for the next ten years, eventually serving on its board of directors and as an officer. But more than that, it was because of the camping experience that I was able to form life-long friendships, encounter mentors who guided me to a career in pastoral ministry, helped me decide which college to attend, and most significantly, meet the girl I was to marry. And all because of a long-forgotten essay. I remind Mary Ann that I actually won her in a contest, for that single entry when I was ten years old set in motion a chain of events that led to our meeting.

There are no accidents in life. Every circumstance has meaning. Some disappointments have turned out to be beneficial, and some successes have brought regret. And yet all of life's occurrences have been learning experiences.

And still, the question of theodicy remains. It is the age-old conundrum of philosophers and theologians: Why does an all-powerful God of love permit the existence of evil? Is it that a loving God is not omnipotent? Or is it that God is not a God of love in that God allows evil to run rampant in our world? Why does evil exist? Why do humans believe they are serving God when they slaughter those whom they believe are the enemies of God?

Yogi Berra was right when he observed, "It ain't over 'til it's over." The creator's human experiment is not yet concluded. We are still in a process of becoming. The apostle Paul noted that through the avatar Jesus of Nazareth, God will reconcile all things to himself, whether on earth or in heaven (Col 1:20). As the universe is expanding, it will also contract, and in the end, there will only be the mind of God of which all things will be part.

Gray Matter, Dark Matter, and Doesn't Matter

The psychologist Carl Jung developed the concept of synchronicity, of meaningful coincidences. Events occur that may have no causal connection yet can affect a result. Neils Bohr and Werner Heisenberg, quantum physicists, also posited the interconnectedness of all things, that space and time are related. If all the events that have occurred within the human drama from the beginning of our existence are related, then the next logical step is to elicit meaning. I will wait for another form of existence to discover what that is.

MIND YOUR OWN BUSINESS

When the philosopher Rene Descartes used the phrase "Cogito, ergo sum," he was attempting to provide evidence for the reality of his own existence. "I think, therefore I am" lays the foundation for one's state of being. In the King James Version of the Bible, the verse from Prov 23:7, "As a man thinketh in his heart, so is he," suggests that the mind determines the form and character of the person.

Your mind is your own business. Your mind shapes who you are. It affects your body and can foster both sickness and healing. Your mind is crucial in your relationships with others. And it determines how you relate to your environment.

When residents of the Golden State talk about a "California state of mind," they are talking about a relaxed and easygoing approach to life, about walking on beaches, savoring sunsets, lingering over your coffee, taking life as it comes, and pausing to meditate.

Unfortunately, most of us do not take the time to stop to think. Our lives seem always to be in a hurry to do the next thing on our agenda. The Gospels often describe the busyness of the life of Jesus. Mark, for example, uses an abundance of the word *eutheos*, meaning "immediately, at once, now." It is no wonder that Jesus often goes off by himself to meditate. He urges his disciples to do the same: "The apostles gathered around Jesus, and told him all that they had done and taught. He said to them, 'Come away to a deserted place all by yourselves and rest a while.' For many were coming and going, and they had no leisure even to eat. And they went away in the boat to a deserted place by themselves" (Mark 6:30–32).

We need times of vacation. And I mean that in the original sense of the word. Vacation means "to vacate"—"to leave empty." Vacation is theoretically that time of renewal when we prepare ourselves for the next cycle of activity by clearing the old slate. It's a washing of the blackboards in preparation for the next lesson. Interestingly, the British refer to vacations as being on "holiday." "Holiday" derives from "holy day"—a sacred time set aside for God, when one thinks about God's presence in one's life. I'm sure the British don't think about holidays being sacred time any more than we think about vacations being times for renewal—but we ought to.

We need the time to quiet the soul and listen to God, especially on those occasions of stress and confusion. We need the time to build a deeper relationship with the God in whom we live and move and have our being. Some seek to do this through formal worship but find it difficult. Our worship services are filled with prayers directed to God, hymn singing and praise, and activity of one sort or another so that we become spectators rather than worshipers, and an audience rather than a congregation. Worship has become performance and entertainment. The element that is missing is silence—silence in which God may speak to us, in which we may, as the psalmist says, "Be still and know that I am God."

When Lobsang Samden introduced me to a Buddhist form of mediation, I found it to be very relaxing, mind-clearing, as well as a form of ecstasy. The Dalai Lama's brother did not talk a lot, but what was in his mind communicated in other ways, and I saw the effectiveness of meditation. After college, I explored Maharishi Mahesh Yogi's Transcendental Meditation and went on to purchase more than a dozen books on how to meditate. What I discovered was that there were just too many words. And yet, beyond the words there lay a truth that formed within my mind. I think of Paul Simon's prophetic words in the sound of silence.

Communication takes place on different levels, but often we must be still and silent in order to process it.

In Buddhist thought, all minds are one mind. Every religion seeks ways to communicate, or be at one with, this universal mind or God. Consequently, virtually all religions have developed ways to enter into this universal mind by recognizing the God within. Hindus, Jainists, Buddhists seek to attain *samadhi*, a state of meditative consciousness through various methods of meditation. Eastern Christians practice "Hesychasm," a contemplative monastic tradition that involves asceticism or isolation. Sufis, the mystical branch of Islam, seek to purify the inner self so that they can be worthy. Native Americans, like the Celts, believe that the spirit of the creator inhabits all things and that the individual connects with the divine by practicing mindfulness through meditation, prayer, and ceremony.

One of the current scientific breakthroughs is "dream engineering." It appears to be a form of subconscious mindfulness in which external stimuli, such as fragrances, are introduced just prior to, and during sleep. Scientists are experimenting with dream-induction devices that use sounds or electrodes to affect the mind of the dreamer and therefore change the attitude and mind of the sleeper.

The practice of mindfulness is very much in vogue these days, and there are many practitioners who teach a variety of methods and techniques. Mindfulness is mediation in which you focus on being intensely aware of what you're sensing and feeling in the moment, without interpretation or judgment. Lobsang emphasized mindfulness through concentration on breathing since the breath was the divine spirit that is a part of all living creatures. We breathe in the love of God; we breathe out God's love for all. I often use concentration on certain images of the mind to calm both body and mind.

To be alive, to be conscious, is to be aware, to know who you are in relation to your world and to one another. We need to take time to mind our own business of living well.

"ONE HAND CLAPPING"

Physics was not one of my favorite high school subjects, mostly because of the math. Sitting in Mr. Brinn's classroom one afternoon, he caught me off-guard when he said, "Serio, what is the sound of one hand clapping?"

Of course, it was a well-known Zen koan, but I didn't know it then. I just sat there and stared at the teacher. "Well, do you have an answer?" Finally, I said, "Yes, and I just gave it to you." Silence. A Zen master would say, "If you understand what I am saying, you are wrong."

The origin of the universe may be difficult to understand, and if you do understand it, you are probably wrong. We assume that the universe began in silence. And then with movement, vibrations coalescing into infinitely small particles moving at various frequencies, and over billions of years of trial and error formed particles that came together into various states of matter. Science may be able to explain the evolutionary process. It cannot explain the intelligent design behind it. Science must defer to religious faith.

We are sound. The universe is a harmonic frequency. Every atom, reduced to its subatomic particles—quarks, leptons, gluons, mesons, photons, bosons, fermions, etc.—further reduced are simply vibrations.

It is interesting that many religions believe that a divine entity began the process of creation. The holy book of Judaism and Christianity begins with a formless void out of which God says, "Let there be light." The thought of God becomes the thing itself.

The Gospel writer John, a proponent of "Logos theology," writes, "The Word became flesh" (John 1:14). Spirit takes on form. That which cannot be seen becomes visible. God becomes human. Jesus of Nazareth is the manifestation of the cosmic energy that formed the universe. And so are we all.

If all the cells of our body are vibrational, then sound affects the body. Don Campbell, in his book *The Mozart Effect*, describes how music is used to heal the body and affect the mind's ability to deal with one's environment. Sound waves, often in the form of ultrasound, are increasingly being used in medicine to restore damaged cells and to foster the healing of wounds. The brain and central nervous system consist of white matter and gray matter which control the body's function and thinking ability. The nerve bundles that connect these cells are sheathed with myelin. Scientists have found that sound waves can restore damaged myelin and aid in myelinogenesis. Neuroscientists are also finding that the practice of mindfulness can also restore and heal the brain and the heart.

In my book *The Mysticism of Ordinary and Extraordinary Experience*, I have a chapter on the "Mysticism of Jazz." Quoting from the opening paragraphs, I wrote:

> The material world that we think is so solid, when reduced to its atomic structure, is simply energy vibrating at different frequencies. We are sound and when we use such expressions as "resonating to ideas," "feeling bad vibes," "living in harmony," or "getting in tune with . . .," we are using the language of our basic nature and how the universe is structured. It is interesting that even the word *music*, which is the art of arranging sounds, is related to *muse*, "to think creatively."

(You may want to take a look at Joachim-Ernst Berendt's book, *The World Is Sound: Nada Brahma: Music and the Landscape of Consciousness*.)

To the Hindu and Buddhist, one achieves unity with the cosmos through sound. *Nada* is the Sanskrit word for "sound," and Brahma is one of the three personifications of God. The expression

Gray Matter, Dark Matter, and Doesn't Matter

"Nada Brahma" means "sound is God" and "God is sound." This concept influenced the music of Ravi Shankar and Philip Glass, who have used a form of jazz to induce a kind of cosmic consciousness. Philip has periodically given concerts at the church where I was pastor, and his music has always been transformative and meditative.[1]

We do, indeed, resonate with different frequencies and thereby add to the music of the spheres and the greater harmony of the universe. A man I much admire, the transcendentalist Henry David Thoreau, in his conclusion to *Walden*, said, "If a man does not keep pace with his companions, perhaps it is because he hears a different drummer. Let him step to the music which he hears, however measured or far away."

An answer to the Zen master who asked what is the sound of one hand clapping may be to go within oneself and listen to the music of your soul as you interact with all that is.

---

1. Serio, *Mysticism of Ordinary and Extraordinary Experience*, 131.

THE PSI FACTOR

There was a time when people believed that the world was flat. You couldn't blame them, though. They believed what they saw. They looked at the surrounding countryside and it looked flat. When they went to a neighboring town, they went over mountains and into valleys, but they appeared to be traveling on a level plane. The sensory evidence they had accumulated from the land on which they lived told them that the Earth was flat.

Then someone, perhaps someone living near the sea, made a new observation. He noticed that when a ship sailed out from shore, the hull first slipped below the horizon, and slowly the sails followed until the entire ship was below the line of sight. Could it be that the Earth was round like a ball? While the ancient Greek philosopher Pythagoras, around 500 BCE, observed a lunar eclipse, speculating that it was the Earth's shadow on the moon and saw that it was round, it may have been hard to convince the unlearned common person.[1] Then, Ferdinand Magellan's crew sailed west and came back to the point from which they started, and the skeptics were convinced.

The frontiers of our knowledge have been rapidly changing ever since. Who would have thought even fifty years ago that it would be possible to have the entire contents of the Library of Congress sitting on one's desk in the form of electrons stored on a hard drive and eventually in bio-electronic molecules that would

---

1. Aristotle, around 350 BCE, stated that the Earth was round, as did Aristarchus, and Eratosthenes was able to measure the circumference of the Earth.

be self-replicating? Most of us can remember a time when having access to all the information in the world through something called the Internet was pure science fiction. My grandmother would have thought that preparing a meal in a microwave was nothing less than sorcery. If we have learned anything in recent history, it is to be careful in the use of the word "impossible."

When it comes to the analysis of the Bible, we seem to adopt a different method of reasoning. At one end of the spectrum are those who maintain that the incredible events in the Bible are simply myth and fable, stories invented to convey spiritual truths, or they are the interpretations of primitive minds that have become distorted in their retelling over the centuries. Or perhaps, as the theologian Rudolph Bultmann suggests, biblical events have a perfectly logical explanation, and that the Bible is not about God but about the human understanding of God.

At the other end of the spectrum are those who say that everything in the Bible occurred exactly the way the Bible says it did, that God allowed miraculous events to occur two to four thousand years ago because they were necessary to establish our religious faith and that we simply have to believe that they did happen. We could go off on that philosophical tangent and say that all reality is a matter of faith, of trusting in our own observations and the evidence that others present. We construct our own reality, and sanity is nothing more than shared illusions.

I have never been to Maui, but I believe that it exists. I know some people who have been there, and I believe them when they describe it. I would also be inclined to trust the mapmakers and even satellite photos, although it's possible they could be fabricated. I suppose I could even go there, but if I did, how could I be sure that someone wasn't trying to trick me by putting up the wrong sign at the airport? Eventually, though, I would gather so much evidence, so many signs and indications that I would believe that Maui exists. Or I could simply accept its existence and go there and enjoy the beach, whether it was real or not.

On the other hand, if someone I had known years ago and who had died would suddenly appear in my living room and began talking to me about my future, I think I would react differently. After all, people do return from Maui, but they seldom return from the dead. In that case, I would wonder if it was an actual ghost or a figment of my imagination, or if there would be any difference. You may remember that scene from *Macbeth* when he says,

> Is this a dagger which I see before me,
> The handle toward my hand?
> Come, let me clutch thee. I have thee not, and yet I see
> thee still.
> Art thou not, fatal vision, sensible to feeling as to sight?
> Or art thou but a dagger of the mind, a false creation,
> Proceeding from the heat-oppressed brain?[2]
>   (*Macbeth*, Act II, Scene 1)

Is what we see and hear always that which exists, or is it a creation of the brain, a reality constructed based on the sensory information supplied to it?

In the Old Testament, the boy Samuel hears voices in the night. The priest Eli does not hear them, but after being awakened three times, he is wise enough to know that the boy is experiencing clairaudience—hearing sounds that are not produced by sound waves. Eli knows the cause of this. He tells Samuel, "Go, lie down; and if he calls you, you shall say, "Speak, Lord, for your servant is listening" (1 Sam 3:9). The text tells us that in those days people were not accustomed to hearing God and that even visions were not widespread. Dreams, the so-called "dark speech of God," were also not present. But now we have a child who has extrasensory perception and hears voices that appear to be human. Samuel has an extraordinary gift to discern another dimension of reality of which many of us choose to be oblivious. We are too accustomed to living in Flatland to believe that the world is round. We will not accept the existence of a spiritual dimension or that there can be any communication from that dimension, whether of ghosts or of God.

The Gospels also have cases of clairvoyance. When the disciples try to persuade Nathanael to join their group and follow Jesus, he asks sarcastically, "Can anything good come out of Nazareth?"

---

2. Shakespeare, *Globe Illustrated Shakespeare*, 2009.

Then Jesus arrives and tells Nathanael that he is one who speaks his mind. Nathanael wonders how Jesus can know anything about him before meeting him. Jesus says, "I saw you under the fig tree before Philip called you" (John 1:46–48).

The Bible tells us that Jesus possessed many abilities which we would regard as psychic. In addition to clairvoyance and clairaudience, he also had the gifts of telepathy, psychokinesis, and therapeutic touch, the ability to communicate with spirits, levitation, bilocation, as well as the ability to project his spirit out of his body and to raise the dead. If we believe that Jesus was able to perform these miracles, then we should also believe Jesus when he says that we can do them as well.

The ability to perform miracles has always been regarded by the church as an indication that one has a special relationship with God. Indeed, the Roman Catholic Church requires at least two substantiated miracles before one is named a saint. Many of the Christian mystics had these special gifts, but they were never their ultimate goal. The mystical experience was sought in order to experience the presence of God and to enjoy the overwhelming love of God. Persons who seek to develop psychic abilities miss the point entirely—they desire the sign instead of that to which the sign is pointing. The map is not the terrain. As Jesus said, "But strive first for the kingdom of God and his righteousness, and all these things will be given to you as well" (Matt 6:33). When you have experienced the love of God, you will not want anything else.

Francesco Forgione was born in a small Italian town in 1887. He entered the priesthood and demonstrated an intensity of religious devotion. In 1918, after a celebration of a Mass commemorating Saint Francis's reception of the stigmata, Padre Pio, as he was now called, wakened the next morning from an ecstatic state of union with God that left him on the floor of the choir bleeding profusely from his hands, feet, and side. These wounds never healed during the remaining fifty years of his life.

Kept under virtual house arrest by the church, which did not take kindly to miracles that they could not explain, Padre Pio nevertheless developed a following. Stories of healings attributed to him, visionary appearances made to people in turmoil, and the wisdom of his teachings became legion. The Catholic Church canonized Saint Pio in 2002.

We use the word "miracle" to describe an unbelievable occurrence. NFL football must be a spiritual experience for many, perhaps because much of it occurs on a Sunday. It reminds me a little bit of church sometimes when I see those committee meetings followed by short bursts of activity. Football also uses religious terminology to describe some fantastic plays like a "Hail Mary pass" or an "Immaculate Reception." Philadelphia Eagles fans remember the Miracle of the Meadowlands. I suppose this is a legitimate use of the word since the word "miracle" comes from the Latin meaning "to look at in wonder." A miracle is therefore anything that excites our amazement. However, in a religious sense miracles are events for which physical causes cannot be determined, and secondly, they are beyond the ordinary causation of humans.

Miracles, or the psi factor, are evidence for the existence of another realm, a spiritual world, that lies beyond us and within us, and that interpenetrates our own in many ways. In times of quietness and prayer, in times of desperation and seeking, in those times when we are most in need of God and feel God's absence intensely, those are the times when heaven draws close to us and we become aware that the world is larger than we think it is.

When God calls in the silence of the night, be still and know that God is with you and within you. In an age of science and technology when we are reaching out to the farthest limits of the universe, let us remember that the greatest undiscovered territory is the human heart. It is in our relationships with one another that we will discover the presence of God.

THE PARANORMAL
AND THE CHURCH

In 2006 I was elected president of the Academy of Spirituality and Paranormal Studies (currently named the Academy of Spirituality and Consciousness Studies.) This is an academic society whose well-known members studied such matters as post-mortem survival and the frontiers of human consciousness. Its advisory council included such persons as Larry Dossey, Raymond Moody, Jean Houston, Stanley Krippner, Lawrence LeShan, Gary Schwartz, Charles Tart, and other researchers.

Michael Tymn, editor of the academy's journal, interviewed me at the beginning of my term. I include an excerpt here as it reflects some of my beliefs at the time regarding the paranormal and religion.

The Rev. Dr. Harry L. Serio is not the stereotypical Christian minister. The pastor of St. John's United Church of Christ in Kutztown, PA, Serio takes a liberal view of Scripture and is very much interested in paranormal phenomena. His doctoral work at Lancaster Theological Seminary was in the field of Christian mysticism.

As a biblical archaeologist, Serio did research at the University of Pennsylvania on the Royal Tomb of Gordium (Anatolia) and has studied archeology in Italy, Greece, Turkey, and Israel. He was elected president of the Academy of Spirituality and Paranormal Studies, Inc. during June.

In a recent e-mail interview, Serio responded to questions about his beliefs.

How do members of your church and your Christian colleagues react to your interest in the occult? If "occult" is a "dirty" word, should we better call it the supernatural or the paranormal?

"As we know, words are signs that point to meanings beyond themselves. One word by itself is imprecise, so we must always ask a person what is meant by the choice of a particular word. 'Occult' has a lot of negative baggage. Its original meaning was 'secret' or 'hidden' and therefore 'beyond our comprehension.' However, its common usage implies an association with demonic forces. Therefore, I have chosen not to use it. My congregation and colleagues are aware of my interest in 'mysticism,' the direct awareness of ultimate reality. Mystics, in seeking this union with God, often experienced what we would call paranormal phenomena. I even hesitate to use the term 'supernatural,' since any event that occurs or is perceived in the natural world is not beyond it but part of it. 'Paranormal' is the better word, since, even though its connotation is beyond the normal, its original definition is alongside normal experience.

"Those who know me know that my interest in paranormal events is not only scientific, but also a search for meaning or relevance. It is interesting to note that those who witnessed the miracles of Jesus didn't ask how he did them, but rather, what did it mean that he was able to perform these apparent contradictions of nature.

"While many of my colleagues have referred parishioners to me to perform exorcisms or counsel them on paranormal events which they have experienced, this has not been a primary focus of my ministry and therefore has not been an issue of concern."

Have your studies of paranormal phenomena changed your understanding or appreciation of the Bible?

Gray Matter, Dark Matter, and Doesn't Matter

"The Old Testament is a collection of myths and legends from many sources, along with laws and precepts designed to solidify and establish the Hebrew culture. From this tribal perspective, the Hebrew people perceived a nationalistic God who chose them above all others, who waged war on their behalf and even effected the slaughter of innocent children. We no longer worship a sadistic God who sanctions perjury, prostitution, slavery, and many other reprehensible practices that can be found in Scripture.

"Recognizing that the Bible is a record of how a particular people perceived God interacting in their history, one must also apply that same hermeneutical principle to the interpretation of paranormal events which should not be taken literally but understood in the context of how those descriptions are used. We cannot examine paranormal phenomena in the Bible empirically, nor were they intended to be. They are to be understood metaphorically as signs that point beyond themselves."

Fundamentalist Christians often point to Leviticus 20:6 and 20:27 as well as Deuteronomy 18:12–13 as reasons to steer clear of spirit communication. How can these Old Testament passages be reconciled with 1 John 4:1 or 1 Corinthians 12:10, which tell us we should test the spirits and be discerning of them?

"Fundamentalists pick and choose which portions of Scripture they want to use to support their particular religious practices. If they adhered strictly to biblical injunctions, they would stone their disobedient children and put to death anyone who worked on the Sabbath and refrain from eating pork and shellfish. The same passage that prohibits consultation with wizards and witchcraft also dictates that you can't eat rare meat or get a haircut.

"Spirit communication was prohibited in order to prevent persons from receiving 'unauthorized' direction and to preserve the monopoly of priests and prophets to interpret the will of God. All ancient civilizations had their professional augurs, sybils, and priests who had lucrative practices divining the future and giving advice, and who sought to eliminate the competition. Many of the Israelite kings, including Saul, went outside their culture to consult with Canaanitic mediums. The Deuteronomic code, which was a later revision and reinterpretation of Mosaic laws, sought to centralize worship in one place and eliminate local shrines and practices of the indigenous Canaanite people.

"The apostle Paul argued for discernment in recognizing legitimate direction from spirits, to see if they are of God, that is, if the Holy Spirit is within them. Just because persons are on the other side of this life doesn't necessarily mean that they can offer good advice. Some can be just as stupid and immoral as those who are living in this dimension of being."

How do you interpret Revelation 22:18–21, which suggests, according to many Christians, that the book on truth is closed? If that is the case, why test the spirits and discern what they have to say? Isn't there a conflict there?

"In an age without copyright laws, this is the best that the prophet John could do. There was a similar injunction in Deuteronomy 4:2 against tampering with what has been written. Since the canon of the Bible was not yet formalized, John could only be speaking about his apocalypse and not the entire Bible. George Rawson, 150 years ago, wrote a hymn based on the final words of the pilgrim leader, John Robinson, before his departure to the New World:

We limit not the truth of God to our poor reach of mind —
By notions of our day and sect—crude partial and confined
No, let a new and better hope within our hearts be stirred
For God hath yet more light and truth to break forth from the
Word.

"God is still speaking to us, and in every age we need to discern and apply our understanding of what that means. Truth is a diamond of many facets through which we look, and therefore our interpretation is constantly evolving."

As I see it, the biggest difference between orthodox Christianity and the teachings of spirit since the New Testament relates to the afterlife. Except for the purgatory of Catholicism, Christianity offers us a humdrum heaven or horrific hell, while modern revelation—if we can call it that—suggests an evolution of spirit through many realms. What are your thoughts on that?

"Our theological concepts continue to evolve and change. The Old Testament concept of *sheol* was that of a warehouse of nonconscious souls underneath the earth characterized by darkness, silence, and joylessness, similar to the Greek concept of Hades. It was where one was unaware of the presence of God, even though God is there (Psalm 139:8). Jesus' metaphors for hell were based on a Zoroastrian concept introduced during the post-exilic period. (See my paper on "The Afterlife in the Hebrew-Greek Scriptures," 1999 Proceedings of ARPR, p. 123). The medieval church capitalized on Dante's description of a three-story universe and acquired great wealth and power with its doctrine of the keys. What has changed in all of this is our metaphors for heaven and hell based upon our *weltanschauung*.

"I believe in an evolution of spirit, of continual growth and expansion of consciousness, or awareness of the nature of God. I think the mystics were on target when they said that the goal of existence is ultimate union with God, a bringing together of all the elements of Creation in a cosmic Shalom."

Of course, the atonement doctrine is another big difference. Where do you stand on that?

"Elie Wiesel, in his memoir, *Night*, observed a young boy dying a slow death on the gallows at Birkenau, a victim of the Holocaust. He heard a man ask: 'For God's sake, where is God' And from within me, I heard a voice answer: 'Where is He? This is where—hanging here from this gallows . . .'

"The doctrine of atonement for me is the realization of the divine presence in each of us. Just as God was present in Jesus of Nazareth, experiencing his suffering and death, so God experiences our joys and our pain. Life is a journey to explain the 'why' of existence, and it takes us in two directions: the journey inward to discover who we are as spiritual beings and the journey outward of service in the world that we may experience the magnificent astonishment of living and expressing the love of God in very tangible ways. Our salvation, so to speak, is in knowing that we are loved and that we are not alone in the universe."

"BECOMING A GHOST"

The last words of many people don't always indicate that they know when death is going to happen. Union General John Sedgwick was told by an aide to mind the Confederate sharpshooters. His last words were: "Don't worry. They couldn't hit an elephant at this distance."

Legendary swashbuckler Douglas Fairbanks must have been confused before giving up the ghost in 1939 because his famous last words were "Never felt better."

Crossing the boundary between life in the flesh and life in the spirit involves some adjustment, so we had better prepare for it because we just don't know.

Shortly after the resurrection, the disciples were gathered in the upper room when suddenly Jesus appeared in their midst. "They were startled and terrified and thought that they were seeing a ghost. He said to them, 'Why are you frightened, and why do doubts arise in your hearts? Look at my hands and my feet; see that it is I myself. Touch me and see; for a ghost does not have flesh and bones as you see that I have.' And when he had said this, he showed them his hands and his feet. While in their joy they were disbelieving and still wondering, he said to them, 'Have you anything here to eat?' They gave him a piece of broiled fish, and he took it and ate in their presence" (Luke 24:37–43).

Evidently, according to Luke, the risen Jesus possessed a physical body that could interact with our world. This supports the theory that spirit, the true essence of a person, determines the nature of its body and indeed creates its own body. We know that the mind often affects the healing of the body, but here is a situation where God shows us that a truly developed and advanced spirit such as Jesus can recreate his own body so that those who see Jesus are convinced that he is flesh and blood. This Jesus is a ghost in the flesh or a spiritual body.

Paul addressed the same issue in his letter to the Corinthians when someone asked "In what form will the dead be raised?" Paul's answer: "What you sow does not come to life unless it dies. And as for what you sow, you do not sow the body that is to be, but a bare seed" (1 Cor 15:36–37). What we are now is only an aspect of what we are to be.

Karl Pribram, a researcher at Stanford, has said that the mind stores information and images in holograms. The nature of a hologram is that if you remove part of the structure of the hologram, you do not eliminate part of the picture; you simply degrade it. Everything is there but not as fully formed.

We are now not what we shall be. We are not as fully formed or developed as our spirits are capable of being. Just to give you a hint of the spirit's capability, you may be aware of the body's superhuman ability when placed under extraordinary circumstances: a woman finds the strength to lift a car off her child when normally she can't move a hundred pounds; an Indian fakir prepares his body to walk through a bed of hot coals. What we regard as miraculous is only a fragment of what will be possible in spirit.

Jesus said to his disciples who marveled at his miracles, "You think this is great? You can do this and even more." The life of the spirit holds great potential for us on earth as well as in the afterlife. We are often curious about what will happen to us when we die, not quite believing that there is life beyond the body.

Dr. Susan Muto, who spoke at a conference on spiritual formation that I attended, described her mother's slow deterioration in the Alzheimer's unit of a Pittsburgh nursing facility. As her ability to remember all the precious events of her life was diminishing, her personal history, even who her daughter is, Susan regarded it as a peeling away of one's life as one approached the last stages, a kind of preparation for the crossing over to the next life.

As she talked about her mother going through the final passages of life, I thought of the ancient Greeks who in their mythology believed that the dead would cross five rivers to attain the realm of the afterlife. They included Acheron, the river of pain and anguish; Cocytus, the river of sorrow and regret; Phlegethon, the river of fire that burns away the things of earth; Lethe where all memories are left behind; and finally the river Styx, the last barrier to the land of the dead.

How interesting that Elizabeth Kubler-Ross would also describe five stages of dying, beginning with anger and denial and ending with peace and acceptance. In the Tibetan Book of the Dead, priests assist the dying patient in going through the "*bardos*," the various stages of dying, and the awareness of the next stage of living. The mystic Teresa of Avila, in her vision of "The Interior Castle," goes through several rooms in order to unite with the object of one's eternal quest, the love of God.

Throughout history, and especially most recently, there has been an extensive amount of literature about what happens when a person dies, and most describe a gradual departure from earth and a growing awareness of a spiritual existence. Except for the traumatic or sudden death, a person whose body is deteriorating will go in and out of an awakened consciousness. Dreams will become more real and the awareness of physical reality will diminish until one is more fully aware of the spiritual realm. Here one may encounter a loved one who has earlier made the transition. From the study of near-death experiences and literature from around the world throughout history, there seems to be an entry into a world of light.

Henry Francis Lyte describes it well in his hymn "Abide With Me," when he wrote, "Swift to its close ebbs out life's passing day; Earth's joys grow dim, its glories pass away" and "Heaven's morning breaks, and earth's vain shadows flee."

As our awareness of this life fades, we become more present to the presence of God than to the things of earth. Like Emily in

Thornton Wilder's play, "Our Town," we cannot return to the life we knew because we have moved beyond it. We cannot go home again because the home we knew is no longer relevant when we establish a new residence in another world.

Yes, there are such things as ghosts. In many cases they may be the projections of the human imagination, or as Macbeth suggested, "a dagger of the mind, proceeding from the heat oppressed brain."[1] But they may also be the spiritual projections of those who can't quite leave this earthly scene because of some unfinished business, such as reassuring a loved one that all is well.

Jesus had some unfinished business with his disciples. He wanted to assure them that he had indeed risen from the dead, that there was a continuation of this life in another realm of being, and that the teachings of his ministry were valid and needed to be proclaimed to future generations. Jesus gives us the ability through the mystic vision to peer into the spiritual world.

Jesus wanted his disciples to know that their job was to be present to the moment in which they lived. We should not be overly concerned about the next life but live the life that we are meant to live now. If we are faithful unto death in this world, we will receive the crown of righteousness in the next.

Perhaps Douglas Fairbanks was right after all when he said at the moment of death, "I never felt better."

---

1. Shakespeare, *Globe Illustrated Shakespeare*, 2009.

"WILL YE NO COME
BACK AGAIN?"

A San Francisco raconteur was once asked about his belief in
reincarnation and replied, "I didn't believe in reincarnation
in any of my other lives. I don't see why I should have to believe in
it in this one."

There are some things that exist by believing in them and
others that exist despite our beliefs. A survey by the Pew Forum on
Religion and Public Life (December 2009) reports that 24 percent
of all Americans believe in reincarnation (28 percent for Catholics, a number much greater than a previous poll).[1] Those numbers
seem to be increasing to where one-third of Americans now believe that they will be born again. What the survey does not show
is why people believe in reincarnation. What evidence or rational
process helps to shape one's belief?

Jim B. Tucker, MD has investigated children's memories of
past lives and found that those children whose previous personalities died violently were more likely to remember a past life.[2]

The scientific studies by Tucker, Ian Stevenson, and others
have been accepted as legitimate by many, but they have also been
refuted by persons like James Webster. It always comes down to a
matter of faith, whether it's belief in reincarnation as a religious
principle or belief in the legitimacy of empirical studies.

1. "Majorities of U.S. Adults."
2. Tucker, *Life before Life*, 92–93.

My own encounter with reincarnation occurred when I attended a gathering of persons who were listening to a discarnate entity named Katrinka ("Katey") Knockstead who spoke through a trance medium. Those in the group were asking about previous lives and received a variety of answers ranging from nuns to witches, philosophers to royalty. When it became my turn, I expected something profound and exciting but was told simply that in my last incarnation, I had been a dirt farmer in Idaho in the nineteenth century.

I asked Katey, "Wasn't I anyone of historical note, someone whom I could check out?" Of course, a thousand people have claimed to be Napoleon, or Abraham Lincoln, or other well-known celebrities of the past. Katey paused and then said, "Well, you had been Philip Yorke, the first Earl of Hardwicke." I had no idea who that was and I was sure that the retired postal worker who was channeling Katey would have less of an inkling.

From childhood I have had a fascination with Celtic stories, read many of the novels of Sir Walter Scott, and, later became interested in Celtic spirituality. What a surprise it was to learn that Philip Yorke was the English jurist who sentenced many of the Jacobite rebels to be hanged after the battle of Culloden. Even though I believed Bonnie Prince Charlie to be a pompous blaggard, there was still the romantic story of Flora MacDonald rowing him over the sea to Skye. Hardwicke would have been delighted to lay his hands on the cowardly prince.

Was the medium reading my mind, and how could this uneducated man come up with such an obscure name? There were many questions. It was an interesting experience, but it certainly wasn't definitive proof.

There are many other anecdotal accounts suggestive of reincarnation—hypnotic regression to pre-birth existence: children, from Shanti Devi to James Leininger (*Soul Survivor*), who remembered previous lives; the tale of Bridey Murphy that was entertaining but not taken too seriously, and the birthmarks that Ian Stevenson reported in his studies that may have been indicative of past-life trauma. It is interesting, but is it proof?

Gray Matter, Dark Matter, and Doesn't Matter

The belief in reincarnation was certainly present in the early church. Origen, Synesius, and other church fathers were known as the *Pre-existiani*, maintaining that the soul existed before its present incarnation. Others believed that the soul could be incarnated again. The doctrine of reincarnation was rejected by the Council of Constantinople in 553 as incompatible with the Christian faith. It was a political move orchestrated by Emperor Justinian and his wife, Theodora, a devout Monophysite, that removed the doctrine from the canons of the church.

Today there are many persons who believe in reincarnation because it makes sense to them and answers many of the questions relating to the mystery of life and the "why" of our being.

THE BLOB

Every summer the Colonial Theater in Phoenixville, Pennsylvania, holds a "Blobfest" to commemorate the 1958 B-movie *The Blob*, which was filmed in the town. *The Blob* is not a great movie and would not compare to other alien visitation films of the same era, although it could serve as a metaphor for overindulgent eaters who pig out on any type of food. *The Blob* is about an amoeba-like extraterrestrial who comes to Earth and consumes everything in its path, expanding its size as it devours all living things.

What made the film of special interest to us was Mary Ann's meeting with Steve McQueen, the actor who was playing his first lead role. Mary Ann was a teenager and the supply organist at the Hungarian Reformed Church on Main Street. She had just finished practicing and was leaving the church when she saw much commotion with many people and cameras across the street. She sat down on the church steps to observe what was happening. McQueen saw this attractive teen and crossed the intersection to sit down next to her. She asked him what was going on, and he replied ever so casually, "Oh, we're just making a film." The scene they were shooting was at Dr. Hallen's office on the corner of Third and Main, which was an actual physician's office.

Mary Ann had no idea who she was talking with. McQueen appeared to be just a random teenager who looked quite young, although he was twenty-eight years old at the time. Had she been aware of the fame he was to achieve she would have asked for his

41

autograph. He asked her if she wanted to be in the movie. They were going to film a crowd scene of people rushing out of the Colonial to escape the Blob. Mary Ann went down to the theater the next day and saw a sign on the door asking for those who wanted to be in the crowd. At that point, she decided that she didn't want to be in the film. Stardom can be so elusive.

The Colonial Theater was very familiar to us. There was a dance studio on the third floor of the building where Mary Ann went for lessons as a child. When we were dating, the Colonial was a regular haunt since Bridge Street extended to Collegeville where I was a student at Ursinus College. We saw many movies there, and the greasy floor of the theater (from so many spilled drinks and candy and popcorn residue) reminded us of the Blob oozing its way out of the movie house.

The annual Blobfest includes a "Run-Out" event at the Colonial with many teens seeking to escape the Blob. The pseudo-panic reminds me of that time during the Fifties when many monster movies were being made and the culture was intrigued by the possibility of an alien invasion. World War Two was over, but it had been replaced by the communist threat, fear of nuclear war, as well as creatures from outer space. We all learned to say the words *"Klaatu barada nikto."*

Compared to all the other cinematic aliens and monsters, the Blob is appealing since it is non-anthropomorphic with no discernable intelligence, and it doesn't try to communicate. It just is. We don't know whether it is conscious, having awareness of itself, since it indiscriminately consumes all biological matter and integrates other life forms into itself. Perhaps Richard Dawkins and Neil deGrasse Tyson are onto something when they speculate that this may be the way life evolves. We exist in a living universe, and life has infinite permutations.

The Blob's weakness was discovered when the characters Steve and his girlfriend took refuge in a walk-in freezer and the Blob retreated from the cold. Steve also learned that CO_2 fire extinguishers also worked. Armed with extinguishers from Mary Ann's nearby school, the Blob was immobilized and was loaded onto a military plane and sent to the Arctic. The film ends with a large "?" Now, seventy years later, we may have a new threat from global warming as we wait for the monster to come in from the cold.

APPARITION WITH
A MISSION

For thirty years we vacationed annually at Wrightsville Beach, North Carolina. I remember the first time we pulled off I-95 onto Rt. 117. It was after dusk and the road would take us through such small towns as Magnolia, Burgaw, and Rose Hill. Most of the road passed through wooded areas and tobacco fields. What impressed me was the number of signs, mostly hand-written, with Bible verses and the message "REPENT" or "JESUS IS COMING SOON." But what really stood out in my recollection was a large billboard set some distance away from the road with the words "United Klans of America" and the dreaded burning cross.

A few years later the Ku Klux Klan sign had been taken down, but the last time we traveled that road, Jesus was still coming. Of course, Jesus' arrival has been imminent for the last two thousand years, and I am sure that his appearance will be met with the same reaction as those first disciples who were startled and terrified and thought that they were seeing a ghost, except for North Carolinians who believe that Jesus was one of their own. He must have been a redneck since he attended a fish-fry on the beach (John 21:9–14).

The question is: who was it that appeared on the beach and seemingly ate fish and demonstrated his corporeal nature to his unbelieving followers? After all, ghosts do not have breakfast, and a ghost does not have flesh and bones . . . but do they?

We are the ones who are doing the perceiving, and we see what our minds tell us to see; we feel what our minds tell us to feel. Perhaps the perception of Jesus was in the minds of the beholders.

When the philosopher-psychologist Julian Jaynes published his landmark book, *The Origins of Consciousness in the Breakdown of the Bicameral Mind*, he created quite a stir with his theory that human consciousness is only three to four thousand years old. He said that the ancient peoples did not think the way we do. The unseen visions and unheard voices were in actuality the right side of the brain speaking to the left but interpreted as coming from some external deity. Some sort of catastrophe occurring in antiquity forced humans to learn how to be aware of their environment and their place in it. In other words, we became self-conscious and aware of who we are.

It is interesting how in the evolution of human life we separated from the rest of the animal species. We became anxious, aware of our finitude, aware that one day we will die. We adopted behaviors unknown in the rest of the animal kingdom. Chipmunks don't have to deal with their dark side. Cats are not suicidal. Squirrels do not mobilize to engage in war on other squirrels. And dogs do not appear to need alcohol to unwind at the end of the day.

Only humans have the capacity to imagine, to create, to prepare for future needs or dangers, or to contemplate the meaning of existence. Only our species postulates a creator, the continuation of life beyond this one, or the relevance of a purposeful life. Only humans have a sense of God.

Sigmund Freud in 1927 published a monograph, *The Future of an Illusion*, in which he said that various religions were nothing more than emotional thermostats to regulate human fears and anxieties. God was the response to the trauma of self-awareness. Many others have suggested that the need for God will diminish as human consciousness continues to evolve. Or at least our concept of who or what God is. God is an illusion that will eventually dissipate.

Is all this accidental? Did we just happen to come into being in some mysterious way? Or are we the result of a God beyond ourselves, a collective unconscious or super-soul?

The post-resurrection appearances of Jesus speak to this question of who we are and what our purpose is. When Jesus appeared on the beach, it wasn't to help the disciples go surfing for answers. He invited them to look, touch, taste, hear, to use their senses to perceive the reality of what was happening. There was a plan for what was occurring. There was intentionality. All these things were done to fulfill that which was written and spoken of and were in the subconsciousness of the culture.

We are children of a creator God. The divine resides within us. Jesus said, "The realm of God is within you" (Luke 17:20-21). When all humanity becomes aware of this God-nature, that we are intended to be expressions of *agape*-love—God-love—then the realm of God will be manifest on this earth.

In the meantime, we need to do those things which give expression to the God within us. This does not happen when we make war upon one another, when we destroy our own habitat, or when we kill ourselves through self-destructive behaviors such as substance abuse.

We become godlike when we follow the example of Jesus and find ways to express God's love and creative power to all people. Whether it is something simple like cleaning up our environment, demonstrating love and concern to victims of cancer, or arousing the creative spirit in our souls to produce or enjoy the arts, our mission in its larger scope is to be what God intended us to be.

Jesus came to make us aware of that and to reestablish the connection between ourselves and our creator. The apparition had a mission at the fish fry and that was to instill a sense of community among the disciples and to point them to a larger purpose beyond themselves. Eating with his friends, breaking bread, and drinking wine, is communion, an act of including all in the larger fellowship of God's family. For this reason, no one is excluded, and no one is left out in the cold. All are welcome at Christ's table. It is collectively that we are one with our God, for in the end all things will be reconciled to God through the awareness of the Christ-spirit in each of God's children.

NAMING THE DEVIL

Christians, as well as adherents of many other religions, believe in a deity that has created all that there is. The apostle Paul says that the Christ spirit, the same spirit that was in Jesus of Nazareth, is the means of this creation: "He is the image of the invisible God, the firstborn of all creation; for in him all things in heaven and on earth were created, things visible and invisible, whether thrones or dominions or rulers or powers—all things have been created through him and for him" (Col 1:15–16).

The Christ is the incarnation of the love of God which is the reasoning behind creation, as if a reason is needed. Because of love, God created the universe and is present within it. The corollary to this is that where there is no love, God is not present, and when God is not present, evil prevails. And so when God speaks through the prophet Isaiah and says, "I form light and create darkness, I make weal and create woe; I the Lord do all these things (Isa 45:7), the creation of woe is made by the absence of light and love. The King James Version of the Bible says that God "makes peace and creates evil." The Hebrew word for "evil" that is used can also mean "adversity, affliction, calamity, distress, misery, woe." By endowing humans with free will, we are given the possibility of ignoring the power of love.

Although God says that he is the author of evil, this negative force is created when love is absent. However, God is reported as instituting acts of violence and murder: "Thus says the Lord, I will indeed bring disaster on this place and on its inhabitants" (2 Kgs

22:16). Older versions of the Bible use the term "evil." Is this the same God that the psalmist called on to avenge Israel against the Babylonians when he said, "Happy shall they be who take your little ones and dash them against the rock!" (Ps 137:9)?

Humans have often invoked the blessing of God upon deeds that a loving God would surely condemn. The United States Pledge of Allegiance states that the American nation is "under God, with liberty and justice for all." Yet the history of this country is fraught with activity that this God would not condone. According to this belief, God endorsed the massacre of Native Americans and the appropriation of their lands, the enslavement of African Americans and their later relegation to second-class citizenship, and the invocation of God's blessings upon the selection of leaders of questionable morality and judgment. Under what kind of God does this nation or any nation exist?

We humans have a propensity for blaming others for our moral shortcomings. The ancient religions developed a plethora of deities and demigods who were responsible for afflicting the human race, usually by so-called "enlightenment" and the desire to be godlike. In the Bible, it is tasting the fruit of the tree of the knowledge of good and evil, so that we feel guilty when we have committed a moral sin. "Who told you that you were naked?" asked God of Adam and Eve. Lucifer, whose name means "light-bearer," is alluded to in Isa 14:12 when he is referred to as "Day Star, son of Dawn" who is cast out of heaven. This fallen angel may have some similarity to the Greek Prometheus (meaning "forethought") who steals fire from the gods to benefit humans with knowledge and technology. His punishment is to be chained to a rock where the eagle of Zeus devours his liver, the seat of emotions, each day only to grow back overnight. When will we ever learn?

The devil has many names. A few years ago a prominent homileticist led one of our clergy convocations which she entitled "Sermons from Scratch." It was obvious that she meant the preparation of sermons from nothing, or from the beginning. During one of the breaks, I reminded her that Scratch was another name for the devil. I didn't think she meant that we ought to use the devil as a starting point for sermons.

Stephen Vincent Benet, who wrote *The Devil and Daniel Webster*, refers to "Old Scratch" who makes a deal with farmer Jabez Stone. When the Old Scratch comes to collect, Jabez hires Daniel Webster to defend him. Scratch, which incidentally comes from an Old Norse word meaning "a wizard, goblin, monster, or devil," is the one who deceives, who tries to blur the distinction between the right course of action and the wrong one. The devil, or Satan, as he is sometimes called, is the one who lures us, and deceives us, by offering easy answers, easy solutions, and easy results by taking the path of least resistance and doing the expedient thing rather than taking the harder path.

Old Scratch, Old Nick, Mephistopheles, Beelzebub, Moloch, Asmodeus, etc.—the devil has many names and many incarnations. One of the names that the Bible uses for the personification of evil, or the devil, is Satan. Satan is a "fallen angel," one who comes among mortals to do God's bidding. The term *satan* means adversary, provoker, tempter, or even prosecutor. This "angel of the Lord" appears to Balaam's ass to provoke Balaam to speak to the princes of Balak (Num 22). This angel is a *satan*, but it is really God who is urging his servant to do what he was supposed to do. In the book of Job, one of the oldest books of the Old Testament, Satan is one of the "sons of God" whom God uses to test Job's faithfulness. So Satan is regarded as a servant of God who tests humans. It is Satan who leads Jesus into the wilderness to be tested. Evil is the misuse of the gifts of God. We have personified the nature of evil in the person of the devil who tempts us with greed, power, and pride.

There is a danger in applying human reasoning to divine action. We do not know why things happen the way they do. We can only trust that in the end love will triumph over evil and that the reason for existence will be accomplished. A survivor of Hitler's Holocaust once said that even out of the worst evil that humans can create, some good may eventually come. The universe is in a state of becoming, and the devil may just be part of it.

OPHIDIOPHOBIA

Indiana Jones once fell through the roof of a circus train boxcar and landed in a chest of slithering snakes. He developed a morbid fear of snakes, the technical term being "ophidiophobia."

Snakes have gotten a bad rap through the ages. In the second story of creation in the Bible, the talking serpent, noted for his wisdom, tells Eve that God lied to her. God told Eve, "You shall not eat the fruit of the tree which is in the midst of garden . . . lest you die." The snake convinced Eve that eating the fruit would give her the power of discernment, knowing the difference between good and evil. Her eyes would be open, and she would be like God. In other words, she would become aware of the spirit of God that was already within her.

Donald Englert, my Old Testament professor, often said that the problem of Eden was not the apple in the tree but the pair on the ground. We seem to objectify evil and not admit that it is humans who make decisions that result in evil actions. Theologian Harvey Cox wrote a book titled *On Not Leaving It to the Snake*, indicating the human tendency to avoid responsibility for our actions by casting blame on external forces, including God. Or as Flip Wilson used to say, "The devil made me do it." The serpent in Genesis merely points out an alternative reality for humans.

God, who says that he is the creator of evil (Isa 45:7), uses serpents to punish and kill by afflicting his chosen people: "Then the Lord sent poisonous serpents among the people, and they bit the people, so that many Israelites died." (Num 21:6). But God also uses the snake for healing by telling Moses to put a snake on a pole so those who look at it would be cured. Is this another way of saying that humans have within themselves the power of destruction as well as healing, depending upon which we choose to focus?

It is interesting that in Greek mythology, the snake was sacred to Apollo, the god of healing, and his son, Asclepius, the god of medicine, carried a serpent-entwined rod. This seems to be a cross-cultural symbol adopted by many ancient religions.

The serpent is both good and evil. The Gorgon Medusa had venomous snakes in place of hair so that anyone who would gaze upon her would be petrified, turned to stone, incapable of further action. Cerberus, the three-headed watchdog of Hades, is depicted as having snakes protruding from his body. He was sometimes represented as a poisonous snake. One of the reasons that snakes were connected with the healing arts is that they shed their skin and become renewed. They are also connected with the idea of reincarnation, of beginning a new life.

When I was in the Boy Scouts I learned that there were some 3,900 species of snakes but only four that we should be concerned about in the United States because of their poisonous venom. These were the rattlesnake, coral, cottonmouth, and copperhead. The only one that was prolific in Pennsylvania was the copperhead, and I became afraid that I would encounter one while hiking in the woods at camp. Nevertheless, I came to realize that not all snakes are dangerous, but I must be aware of those that are.

This requires the wisdom of serpents. Did not Jesus tell his disciples, "See, I am sending you out like sheep into the midst of wolves; so be wise as serpents and innocent as doves" (Matt 10:16)? It is said that Saint Patrick drove the snakes out of Ireland. This might be a metaphor for unquestioning loyalty to the church and the acceptance of its dogma without regard to discerning wisdom.

The wisdom of the snake is that we must take responsibility for our own actions, based upon our knowledge. We must learn when harm is inflicted on others that we are also afflicted. We cannot shirk our responsibility by blaming the snake, or the Nazis, or Hamas, or any other expression of evil in our world. We must be wise and we must learn.

NOT IN THE STARS
BUT IN OURSELVES

The Ironbound section in Newark, New Jersey, in the middle of the last century, was predominately German and Italian, with major enclaves of Irish, Polish, and Portuguese. It seemed that in each section there lived an old lady who was adept at foretelling the future. They had their own methods, whether reading cards or palms, or crystal ball gazing.

When I was a young boy delivering newspapers, I had a Romanian family on my route who was downright spooky. I would enter the door next to their storefront apartment and go down a dark hall to their kitchen, passing a door to their parlor. Occasionally it was open and I could see many dark tapestries hanging about. There was a round table in the middle of the room where the babushka-ed old woman would sit with her clients and in her heavily accented speech give them advice on various matters of the heart, business, or family. She was the stereotypical gypsy fortune-teller.

One day my mother came home from work a bit late. She had stopped to have her fortune told. The seer had told her that she would be proud of her three sons, one who would go into a life of service to others, one who would become wealthy, and one who would break her heart. There were other family secrets that were discussed and my mother seemed pleased at what was revealed to her. I don't know if she had gone to see the gypsy or the old Italian woman who used the tarot, or some other diviner.

Gray Matter, Dark Matter, and Doesn't Matter

In addition to scrying (crystal-ball gazing) and reading the tarot, there are other methods of divination. There is the ancient Chinese *I Ching*, the casting of yarrow stalks; astragalomancy, rolling of dice; tasseomancy, reading tea leaves; ornithomancy, watching the flight of birds; palmistry; feeling the bumps on one's head; and so many other forms in different countries used to predict the future and help people make life-altering decisions.

In the Bible, all forms of divination were outlawed by the priests of the Old Testament, presumably because they desired to maintain a monopoly on who speaks for God. They had their own tools for interpreting God's desire for the chosen people. It is said that the high priests had the *urim* and *thummim* on their *ephod* or breastplate. The urim and thummim could have been small stones in a pouch that were taken out and cast, with the priest then interpreting God's message to the seeker.

The most common form of scriptural divination, however, was the interpretation of dreams. Morton Kelsey and John Sanford, in their books on biblical dream interpretation, refer to dreams as "the dark speech of God" and "God's forgotten language." God communicates to prophets, kings, and ordinary people through these visions of the night. From Jacob's ladder to the warnings to the magi, Joseph, and Pilate's wife, God interferes in human affairs through these psychic contacts. God declares that at the end of days when human speech will be no more, "that I will pour out my Spirit upon all flesh, and your sons and your daughters shall prophesy, and your young men shall see visions, and your old men shall dream dreams" (Acts 2:17).

Nevertheless, there are warnings about misinterpretations and deceit: "For thus says the Lord of hosts, the God of Israel: Do not let the prophets and the diviners who are among you deceive you, and do not listen to the dreams that they dream, for it is a lie that they are prophesying to you in my name; I did not send them, says the Lord" (Jer 29:8–9).

Throughout the ages, there have been persons who have been able to prognosticate major events, catastrophes, assassinations, and significant births. Enough errors have been made that call into question that such predictions may be the result of pure chance. Scientists can offer their views on the future based on what they regard as valid reasoning and be terribly wrong. Consider those learned gentlemen who proclaimed that motor cars will never replace horses as a means of transportation, or that humans will never fly, or that atomic energy has very little usefulness. We have not yet learned to be cautious in using the term "that's impossible."

Today, astrology is the most popular form for seeing into the future and predicting events. Astrologers consult the movement of stars to offer advice to seekers. It is believed that at the time of your birth, the stars are in a particular position in the heavens and therefore can dictate the psychological characteristics of individuals and the propensity to act in certain ways.

In Matthew's Gospel, it is the magi, Chaldean astrologers, who see a star and follow it to Bethlehem where the incarnation of God takes place in the birth of Jesus of Nazareth. They are then warned in a dream not to report this to King Herod and return home by an alternate route.

The question most frequently asked is how these signs and predictions take place and who can discern them. We must first recognize that we are all part of the "universe," a word derived from the Latin meaning "to turn as one." All things exist in the mind of God, or, as panentheism maintains, God is present in all things. Carl Jung, the eminent psychologist, used the term "collective unconscious" or a universal consciousness in which we all participate. This also includes the space-time continuum. We tend to think of time as linear, as a sequence of events, one following another. A universal approach is to see all things as one, as a gestalt.

Throughout the history of human civilization there have been certain individuals who possessed the gift of being able to discern greater parts of the whole. We call them prophets, seers, psychics, visionaries, and so on. They are able to have, as the poet John Keats describes, "a peak in Darien" experience. Like the explorer, Balboa, standing on a summit in Panama (Darien) seeing for the first time the Pacific Ocean, he could turn around and see from the same position the Atlantic Ocean. It was as though he could see into both worlds at the same time.

Astrologers may search the heavens, scryers may look into a crystal, tarot readers may turn their cards, but essentially they are looking into their own souls to explore other worlds. In Shakespeare's play *Julius Caesar*, Cassius says, "The fault, dear Brutus, is not in our stars, but in ourselves . . ."[1] Astrology and other forms of divination may be psychological exercises by which persons are able to tap into the collective unconscious and perceive all of existence as one. And this may serve to guide us in the living of our days. What will happen in the future may have already occurred. It is a special gift for some people to be able to perceive that.

A Sanskrit poem written two thousand years ago by the Indian poet Kalidasa sees in each moment of time the totality of all that is meaningful in our lives:

> Look to this day, for it is the very life of life. In its brief course lie all the realities and truth of existence: the joy of growth, the splendor of action, the glory of power. For yesterday is but a memory, and tomorrow a vision, but today well-lived makes every yesterday a memory of happiness and every tomorrow a vision of hope.[2]

1. Shakespeare, *Globe Illustrated Shakespeare*, 1942.
2. Kalidasa, *Look to this day*.

MONKEY ON FIRE

There are people in our lives that we encounter briefly. We never know the full extent of their life journeys, and often the details of their experiences are lost forever. An obituary is but a brief summary and doesn't really provide that which comprises the true essence of a person.

George Kroninger died at the age of eighty-seven. I presided at his funeral. Four years earlier I visited George, and he told me some of his story when he was in the United States Marine Corps between 1922 and 1930. He had served in Haiti, Nicaragua, Hawaii, and twice in China.

While in China, he was attached to the American Legation as a guard, working one day for each three days off. He spoke of one Lieutenant Colonel "Terrible Terry" Williams, later known as the "Bad-Boy General" for his penchant for heavy drinking and bizarre behavior. A strict disciplinarian, he had been forbidden to carry sidearms since on one occasion he fired at a Marine in the ranks for disobeying an order. Instead of being dismissed from the service, Williams was protected by the corp. Evidently, this officer made quite an impression on George.

During George's tour of duty in Haiti, a political faction opposed to "Papa Doc" Duvalier staged a demonstration. A detachment of Marines under Second Lieutenant Blanchard was sent to disperse them. At a river, about 130 feet wide and 1 foot deep, the Haitians were on one side and the Marines on the other. Blanchard ordered the Haitians to disperse, but they proceeded to cross the river. He then ordered a 30-caliber water-cooled BAR mounted on a truck to be fired at their feet. When they continued to cross, Blanchard then gave the order to shoot them. About twenty-five to thirty women and children were killed. A monument with a bronze plaque was later erected on the site listing the names of the dead and indicating that they had been massacred by United States Marines. The monument was toppled a few days later, and no record of the incident has ever been published. George was part of the contingent and was present at the massacre which occurred in August 1929. Although he was only a witness to the killing, George felt that as a member of the corps, he was somehow complicit. His retelling of the incident was almost an act of confession in need of forgiveness.

On another occasion, Marines went into the hills surrounding Port-au Prince and came upon some voodoo practitioners who had prepared a three-foot platter meal consisting of a two-week-old baby that had been roasted and served in the midst of roast plantain, a banana-like fruit. Hearing about this from one of his comrades, George never again complained about his C-rations.

Spider monkeys were common in Haiti and would steal any brightly colored object to take back to their nest. Because of these consistent thefts, the monkeys were hated by the Marines. And because of the Marines' dislike for the Haitians, a few of George's comrades in arms captured a spider-monkey, soaked him with gasoline, set him on fire, and tossed him into the midst of a Haitian village. The inflamed monkey ran among the huts spreading the fire and much confusion. The perpetrators observed from a distance, enjoying the confusion.

As George was telling me these stories I thought of all the unusual and bizarre events that occur in our lives. They may have little impact at the moment but are seared into our memories and may surface in our dreams. The monkey on fire may have been a source of merriment for the warrior band in Haiti, but the residents of that village will remember it in a different way. In each of the incidents that George related, persons acted without thinking of the consequences and how others might be affected. The teachings of Jesus, Gautama, and others direct us to be constantly aware of our thoughts, emotions, and actions on a moment-to-moment basis and especially how they may affect others.

LOST HORIZONS

In the summer of 2023, wildfires completely devastated Lahaina, the main city on the island of Maui in Hawaii, and have had a catastrophic effect on tourism, its principal industry. Over two million tourists visited the island in 2022.

And yet there are people born in Hawaii who spend their entire lives on one island and are buried beneath their native soil without ever having seen even one other island, let alone the mainland of the United States or any other part of the world. So comfortable and lacking in curiosity are they that they seldom wish to know about the world beyond their horizon, much less go visiting.

Having grown up in the shadow of Manhattan's skyscrapers, I can appreciate the sentiment expressed on that well-known cover of the *New Yorker* magazine which featured a New Yorker's view of the world that ended at the Hudson River, beyond which lay the *terra incognita* of New Jersey and the vast wasteland of the rest of the country. I remember when I told some of my cousins that I would be living in Pennsylvania, they expressed their sympathy and wondered how I would survive "out there in the sticks" where there was nothing but corn and cows. Even now when I return for a family gathering I am treated more like a missionary to Africa home on leave.

A lifelong Manhattan resident living in Tribeca was asked for directions to Morningside Heights. He had never been there and had no idea where it was, even though it was only eight miles away. He had heard of Colombia University but didn't know that it was in that section of the city. There are people in the city who have never been to other parts of the cosmopolis.

Lest you think that it's only the cosmopolitan urbanite that has a myopic view of the world, I have met a few people in Berks County, Pennsylvania, who act as though they need a passport to leave the county. They have limited their horizons and refuse to see beyond the fringe of their own existence. A few years ago a Kutztown University student commented on this by posting little stickers around town that read "Kutztown: Life in a vacuum."

It doesn't matter where you live, you can limit yourself by your own perspective. Some people are like that spiritually. They are familiar and comfortable with what they know and believe and seldom wish to push themselves further. They are part of a vast universe, one which is as extensive and overwhelming as the infinite cosmos. But they tend to occupy only a small part of that universe and cannot envision anything beyond their limited horizon.

Horizon is where earth and sky meet. It comes from the Greek word *horus*, meaning "limit." So horizon can mean the limit of a person's vision, but also it has the figurative meaning of the limit of a person's thinking, experience, interest, or outlook. The apostle Paul said of such persons that this world is the limit of their horizon because their minds are set on earthly things (Phil 3:19).

The author of the letter to the Hebrews writes about Abraham who responded to God's call and ventured beyond his physical and metaphysical horizons, "and he set out, not knowing where he was going." It is faith that enables us to see what is not visible (Heb 11:1–12). If you have no vision, no sense of destiny, no purpose in being, you are already dead because you have no place to go since you do not believe that there is any place for you to go. The opposite of death is not life but growth. When you stop growing, you begin dying.

The person of faith does not die because he recognizes that there are no horizons to limit him. He knows that his spirit will not be bound to this world but that he will slip the surly bonds of earth and touch the face of God, as the poet John Magee suggests.

Gray Matter, Dark Matter, and Doesn't Matter

To have that wider view, to see the far horizon that transcends this life enables a person to struggle and endure whatever this life has to offer because he knows there is so much more beyond.

When you grow comfortable with your existence and the world that you occupy, you begin to think that that is all there is. There are elements of the soul that expand the horizons of our vision—such elements as love, wonder, creativity, faith. Without them, we limit ourselves and box ourselves in. One of my favorite poets is Edna St. Vincent Millay, but she can be so depressing at times. She has these lines at the conclusion of her poem "Ashes of Life":

> And life goes on forever like the gnawing of a mouse,—
> And tomorrow and tomorrow and tomorrow and tomorrow
> There's this little street and this little house.[1]

In my early years living in my grandmother's house of four rooms on Marne Street, I was limited only physically, but every room was filled with books that enabled me to think beyond the limited space. (There was even James Hilton's book *Lost Horizons*.) There are many who live in Plato's cave, bound by its darkness, and see only flickering images of reality flashed on the walls of their minds, not realizing the greater reality of a life beyond our knowing, beyond the life that we live.

I was fortunate to be able to escape the limitations of my little house, not only through the pages of my books, but later to travel to more than fifty countries, to live briefly in Europe and work in the Near East, and in the process, to be exposed to different ways of thinking and viewing existence.

Our Christian faith assures us that Jesus of Nazareth came from the creator to help us expand our vision, to recognize our own potential to be fully children of God, to see beyond the horizon of our own mortality to that undiscovered country that awaits our travel. Jesus said, "I am the Way, the Truth, and the Life" (John 14:6). Through him, we enter that vast realm of the spirit. By faith we are assured of what we hope for; by faith, we believe what we do not see. Christ sets us free so that we no longer see the shadows of

---

1. Millay, "Ashes of Life."

existence, but we turn to see the reality of life greater and far more wonderful than we have ever known.

If you want to live in this life as well as the next, push back the horizon that limits you and you will find more than a Shangri-La of eternal youth, you will find yourself free in a world with endless possibilities. You will be able to fulfill your potential as a child of God at one with the universe. You will find yourself a true citizen of the kingdom of God. Christ has set you free, and you are free indeed.

WHEN YOU PRAY

One of the earliest bedtime prayers for children dates back to the eighteenth century. My mother taught me to say this before climbing into bed:

> Now I lay me down to sleep,
> I pray the Lord my Soul to keep;
> If I should die before I wake,
> I pray the Lord my Soul to take.

Of course, at that age, I had no idea what a soul was, but the prayer was somewhat frightening since it led me to believe that I might die in my sleep. Who would want to go to bed thinking you might not wake up?

A few years later when I was attending Sunday school, a kindly superintendent taught us how to pray but not what to say. Fred E. Miller was a crippled elderly man with hearing difficulty who also served St. Stephan's Church as an elder. Apparently he was wealthy since at his death he left an endowment to be used to provide for the theological education of those going into the ministry. To my knowledge, I was the only person from the church to receive money from the Fred E. Miller Student Fund. That and a scholarship from B'nai Brith helped support my seminary expenses. (I may have been the only student to receive assistance from a Jewish organization to enter the Christian ministry.)

Mr. Miller came to our class of first-graders and taught us the posture of prayer. First, bow your head or kneel. This is a sign of submission to God and recognition that you are in the presence of majesty. Then close your eyes to shut out worldly distractions, and then fold your hands so as to eliminate work. You are now ready to communicate with the Almighty.

My Roman Catholic friends taught me that when entering the church, you first anoint yourself with holy water and then proceed to your pew, genuflecting before sitting down. This is "bending the knee." You make the sign of the cross, which is also done when you leave, before and after prayer, when you receive communion, approach the altar, confront a holy icon, at the name of the Holy Trinity, hearing the gospel, and at other times. (I don't know if it helps that much when you come to bat in a baseball game).

It used to be that women, when they went to church, wore hats or a veil as a sign of obedience, but men were obliged to remove their hats, it being rude and disrespectful to cover one's head which was the image of God. The apostle Paul gives a lengthy discourse on this in his letter to the Christians in Corinth (1 Cor 11).

Conservative and Orthodox Jews wear the yarmulke or skullcaps in the synagogue and elsewhere because the Talmud says, "Cover your head in order that the fear of heaven may be upon you."[1] In the same way, Mennonite and Amish women wear their prayer bonnets all the time since Paul says to "pray without ceasing" (1 Thess 5:17), and therefore one is always in a state of prayer.

Occasionally I would take my confirmation class to the local mosque so that they could observe how Muslims engage in *salah*, or prayer, which is performed five times a day. Preparation requires a state of cleanliness, and a room is provided for these ablutions. Special attention is given to the washing of hands, face, and lips as they must be pure when confronting God. Prayer begins with the acknowledgment "Allahu Akbar"—"God is most great." The worshiper faces east toward Mecca where Allah was first revealed to the prophet.

While a student at Ursinus College, I learned that prayer does not necessarily require the speaking of words. My classics professor, Dr. Donald Baker, with whom I had thirty-three semester hours of courses, was a Quaker. He would often invite me to attend

1. Friedmann, "*Kippot* in Jewish Custom."

the Friends Meeting in Phoenixville. Here we sat on hard benches in silence waiting for the Inner Light of God to speak to us so that we could share this enlightenment with others. Too often we had to hear what God was saying to other congregants that I had little time to hear what God was saying to me.

It was another student, Lobsang Samden, the brother of the Dalai Lama and later president of Tibet House, that helped me understand that prayer was not so much speaking, but listening. Quakers and Buddhists, and other religious groups, knew that God was inside of us and that we were expressions of the divine. As several of us would meet in Lobsang's cottage room, we sat seated on the floor in the lotus position, waiting for *samadhi* or enlightenment. At first, I didn't know what to expect. I thought I had to do something. Years later, when Allen Ginsberg was at my church, I heard about his first experience in a Colorado ashram. He expected to go in, meditate, and get inspiration for his poetry. Instead, the monk at the door took his tablet and told him, "No writing. No thinking. Just be."

This exercise of just being—is it a form of prayer? If so, it raises the question of what prayer is and what is it trying to accomplish. Many people would say that it is an attempt to communicate with an intelligent entity beyond the self. But that raises another question: who is listening?

For those who believe in an incarnational and a panentheistic theology, that the creator spirit is in all persons and in all things, then each person is a manifestation of the universal spirit. Prayer, then, is a verbalization of that relation of self to the universe of all that is. Some atheists argue that prayers of petition are an avoidance of responsibility: "Let God do it." There are others who say that prayer is a form of self-actualization. By putting your desires into words, by expressing gratitude for what you deem good in your life, by acknowledging that you are more than who you are, and by recognizing that there is a force that is in control of all things, you are part of a grand design, a cosmic consciousness, and that there is intentionality to creation.

PSYCHOANALYZING GOD

Spring is the time of year, the Bible says, "when kings go out to battle" (2 Sam 11:1). While the world has experienced innumerable armed conflicts in its history, it just doesn't make sense. The annual basketball playoffs have been dubbed "March Madness," but that is a term that might also be applied to the attempts of nations to settle their difference by destroying one another. The world has gone mad every time nations think that war is the answer to peace, as though the only way to make the world a good place is to kill all the bad people.

We live in a world of paradox and insanity. We think we are being reasonable in our thoughts and actions, and we cannot understand when others don't think as we do. We are so sure of ourselves that we are doing the right thing that we really believe that God thinks the way we do and endorses our actions.

Arab children pray to Allah and ask God to deliver them from the Great Satan who wants to kill all Muslims, destroy their culture, enslave their people, and steal their oil, and who believes that God will protect them and finally bring justice by defeating their enemies.

The leader of the free world also knows what is in the mind of God. "Events aren't moved by blind change or chance," said President George W. Bush at a National Prayer Breakfast. "Behind all of life and history, there's a dedication and a purpose, set by the hand of a just and faithful God." And so, as he commits a military invasion force of over a quarter million to the liberation of Iraq, he knows that God is on his side. It is one thing to wage war in a perceived national interest; it is entirely another matter to claim that God endorses it. And that seems to be the issue: how can anyone claim to know the mind of God or to discern the will of the Almighty?

It was Passover, and Jesus went up to Jerusalem, to the great temple, and when he saw how they abused the sanctuary of God's presence, Jesus said, according to Mark's Gospel, "He was teaching and saying, 'Is it not written, "My house shall be called a house of prayer for all the nations?" But you have made it a den of robbers'" (Mark 11:17).

The chief priests and scribes thought they knew what God wanted them to do in God's house. After all, they had read and interpreted the Torah for centuries and had accumulated a body of wisdom in the Talmud, midrash, and halakah. They had poured over every jot and tittle of the law, analyzed the word of God, and knew precisely what God wanted them to do.

And then God's son shows up and tells them that they were wrong. Jesus made some other remarks that they did not understand. Even his disciples couldn't make sense of his words until after the resurrection. The German astronomer Johannes Kepler was right when he said, "O God, I am thinking Thy thoughts after Thee."[1] We can never be sure of the mind of God until they have gone forth to accomplish their work, and even then we cannot be certain when that work is accomplished.

The apostle Paul wrote to the Corinthians, "Where is the one who is wise? Where is the scribe? Where is the debater of this age? Has not God made foolish the wisdom of the world? . . . For God's foolishness is wiser than human wisdom, and God's weakness is stronger than human strength" (1 Cor 1:20). How can anyone make sense of God by using human criteria, let alone declaring that God is in favor of violence and war regardless of its perceived ultimate objective?

Some of my ministerial colleagues and I often differ on how we understand the use of Scripture in psychoanalyzing God or

1. Dao, "Man of Science."

discerning the mind of God. When it comes to understanding the morality of war, which I believe is oxymoronic (there is no such thing as a "holy war"), some are quick to point out the Old Testament passages in which God sends the Israelites out to slaughter their enemies. I have tried to point out that since we are Christians, we are followers of Jesus who calls us to a higher standard of behavior. There is nothing in the Gospels, in the teachings of Jesus, to support the actions of our nation, or any nation, when they take the lives of others. It is human sin that compels war, not divine mandate.

Sometimes Christians are forced to choose between the lesser of two evils. But make no mistake about it, the lesser of two evils is still evil; it is never good. While good people may be compelled by circumstances to act contrary to the principles of their faith, we must never fall into the trap of glorifying the demons of this world. It is in times such as this that we must recognize the frailty of the human condition, fall back upon the grace of God, and in contrition seek divine forgiveness for our complicity in the sins of humankind.

You may have seen the baseball caps and key chains with the initials "WWJD," meaning "What would Jesus do?" That's an appropriate question. "What would Jesus do?" Environmentalists are asking, "What car would Jesus drive?" Today the question is "Who would Jesus bomb?"

The history of civilization is the history of warfare, of nations contending against nations for all sorts of reasons. It is expected of good leaders to protect their country from all enemies, both foreign and domestic. At one time even the pope led papal armies against those whom he perceived as enemies of the church. And there has seldom been a military force representing a sovereign nation or just cause which did not believe that the deity was on their side. Even in the Trojan War, the poet Homer says that the gods and goddesses aligned with either the Greeks or the Trojans.

We still have not learned that God does not take sides in our disputes. Sports teams may invoke the presence of God, but that doesn't mean they are going to win. When Tommy Lasorda's

Gray Matter, Dark Matter, and Doesn't Matter

Dodgers beat the Phillies in the league championship series, Tommy said that God heard his team's prayers. The Phillies' Danny Ozark wondered what happened. His team also prayed. When it comes to discerning the will of God, there clearly is a failure to communicate. Human wisdom is foolishness from God's perspective. The real question that we should be responding to is "Who is the God within me that informs my actions?"

Psychoanalyzing God is not a legitimate human endeavor, for God does not have a psyche that can be analyzed. The ancient Greeks, as well as many other religions, recognized the complexity of the supernatural, that which is beyond the natural. They saw that one deity alone could not contain the complexity of the mind and thought that the aggregate of humans possess. Consequently, they conceived of a pantheon of gods, each possessing a certain quality. If you were ready to go to war, talk to Ares. If you want to fulfill your sexual desires, speak with Aphrodite. If you were ready to embark on a cruise, ask Poseidon for protection. Each god and goddess had a particular domain. In modern times, we have brought about a merger of deities, and so we go within our own consciousness to apprehend the Spirit of the one God within each of us.

Now the question is manifold. Who is the God that dwells within the minds of each person? How do we interpret and make sense of what God may be saying to us? Is God playing tricks on us by giving different messages to Christians, Muslims, Jews, Buddhists, Hindus, etc.? Or is God experimenting with us, using humans to determine what actions work or do not work? Or perhaps the world is one great big classroom in which we all must learn the nature of love through trial and error and learn that the class is not over until it's over, in a time beyond time, in the eschaton?

If the Spirit that is in all humans is, as the New Testament would have us believe, a God of infinite love, then it is not the mind of God that needs to be analyzed but rather our own understanding of the nature of this indwelling God and our interpretation of the intentions of this God.

We indeed walk by faith and not by sight and if we act in this life in a loving and caring way, then the will of God shall be fulfilled and the earth, and the entire universe, shall be reconciled and abide in the peace of its creator.

KIRKRIDGE

The incoming class at Lancaster Theological Seminary in 1963 was required to read the book *Only One Way Left* by George MacLeod. At first, I thought that this was only a political statement and wondered how many ways could one move to the left. After all, this was the sixties, and hippies and beatniks were still advocating their countercultural positions.

I read the book and discovered that George MacLeod had founded the Iona Community on an island off the western coast of Scotland where Saint Columba had created the first abbey and where he subsequently died. MacLeod had previously served at Saint Gile's Cathedral in Edinburgh where his deep interest in social justice continued to develop. His work among the poor and economically disadvantaged in Edinburgh continued at Saint Cuthbert's Church. MacLeod was well positioned on the left side of the political spectrum. In my senior year at the seminary, our class had the opportunity to visit Scotland and see first-hand the work that MacLeod had begun. I couldn't have realized it then but it seemed that I was on a path that was leading toward continued studies in Celtic spirituality and involvement in social justice ministries.

The 1960s were a time when there was a loud demand that the church should break out of its walls and become more visible in all the areas where people interact. The seminary at Lancaster was leading the way with Gabe Fackre's course on the church in society. George MacLeod was arguing that the cross be raised in the marketplace as well as on the church steeple. "Jesus was not crucified in a cathedral between two candles, but on a cross between two thieves."[1]

Celtic spirituality emphasizes panentheism, God's presence in all things. One cannot separate God from the world that God created. This is symbolized by the Celtic cross in the midst of a circle representing the world.

When one examines the life of Jesus of Nazareth it is evident that there is a pattern of retreat from the world and re-engagement in serving the needs of others. The Bible tells us that Jesus often withdrew to a lonely place to commune with God, but then he came down from the mountaintop to teach, to heal, to bring comfort to the oppressed. This was also true of the great mystics of the church who balanced periods of isolation and prayer with a commitment to meeting the needs of society. Some modern mystics such as Dag Hammarskjold and Mother Teresa of Calcutta are good examples of those who saw the relevance of religion to society and practiced a faith in action.

When George MacLeod established the community at Iona and rebuilt the abbey monastery buildings, it was his intention not only to create a community of faith but also to train young people to work in the industrial areas of Glasgow, Edinburgh, and elsewhere in Scotland.

The year that I visited Iona there was a large group of German youth who were practicing the Benedictine principle of "*ora et labora*"—"prayer and work." Following their stay at Iona they would return to Germany and work at various missions in the inner cities. One of the students happened to mention Coventry. Years earlier I had visited the Coventry Cathedral which had been heavily bombed on November 14, 1940, when some five hundred planes of the Luftwaffe reduced the six-hundred-year-old landmark to rubble. In the ruins on the wall behind the altar of reconciliation, charred oak beams were formed into a cross and bore the carved words "FATHER FORGIVE." Below the altar in what had been a coal cellar and an organ chamber, a small international center was

1. MacLeod, *Only One Way Left*, 38.

created where I also met some German students engaged in the work of reconciliation.

There seemed to be a pattern of coincidences in the concept of retreat for prayer and engagement with the world for healing and reconciliation. Following graduation from seminary, I was called to serve a small rural church in Martins Creek, Pennsylvania. I became part of the Bangor Ministerial Association which frequently met at the nearby Kirkridge Retreat Center. The founder of Kirkridge was John Oliver Nelson, who happened to be a friend of George MacLeod and was greatly influenced by him. Kirkridge became a retreat and study center and developed programs on social justice.

I got to know Nelson fairly well. He not only attended our ministerial meetings but would occasionally appear at Sunday worship at my congregation in Martins Creek. He became another one of my mentors. I would also know other Kirkridge directors such as Keith Irwin and Robert Raines and for a time would attend retreats in the hills above Bangor. It was also at Kirkridge that I met John Philip Newell who had served as warden of Iona Abbey.

Philip is also a mystic who hears the sound of God in the pain of the world and encourages the church to respond to God's summons. On the lonely isle of Iona in the Scottish Hebrides he was awakened to the great depths of Celtic spirituality which saw the presence of God in all of creation. Many of his books reflect the growing need for earth consciousness and to "be reminded that the real cathedral of God is the whole of creation." Newell concludes his book *Listening for the Heartbeat of God* with these words: "If the Church's symbols and rituals pointed more clearly to the world as God's dwelling place, we might then more fully rediscover that God's heartbeat can be heard in the whole of life and at the heart of our own lives—if we will only listen."[2]

The Celtic spirit is also alive in nearby Columcille Megalithic Park where stone circles and other stone structures have been erected. It is somewhat reminiscent of the ancient druids who were

2. Newell, *Listening for the Heartbeat of God*, 107.

able to discern the spirit of God in the natural world. It is also a place of meditation and retreat.

Kirkridge is aptly named. "Kirk" is the Scottish word for church, so Kirkridge is the church on the Kittatinny Ridge or a community apart from the world but overlooking the world so as to be re-engaged in the world. It is a place of study and renewal, of losing oneself and finding oneself, of formation and transformation, of reparation and preparation. As Jesus came down from the mountain to be the presence of God in the world, so must we find the time and place to be the Christ to each other.

When it comes to spiritual development and the care of one's soul, the only way to advance is to retreat. Meditation and introspection are necessary processes by which a person can become aware of one's place in the world and discover the reason for one's being. In Buddhism, a three-fold path to enlightenment is described: awareness, understanding or compassion, and community. Kirkridge is a place where that can happen, but each individual must find his or her own special holy ground, a place to be apart and a place to re-enter the social order—and to make a difference for the good of all.

PILGER RUH

Along the Appalachian Trail in Bethel Township, Pennsylvania, where the Tulpehocken Path, now PA 501, crosses it on the Blue Mountain ridge, is a natural spring that came to be known as "*Pilger Ruh*," or "pilgrims' rest." It was an important stopping place for those crossing the ridge. It was visited by Chief Shikellamy of the Iroquois Federation; the Moravian missionary Count Zinzendorff, who settled Bethlehem, Pennsylvania, in 1740; and Conrad Weiser, an interpreter who grew up among the Mohawks, learned their language and customs, and became a trusted scout for George Washington.

Pilger Ruh was more than a resting point at the intersection of two trails. It came to represent the intersection of two cultures—that of the German pioneers who moved into the Tulpehocken area of central Pennsylvania from Schoharie, New York, and the Native Americans of the Lenni Lenape who offered peaceful coexistence. To wander back upon these trails is to remember why those early pioneers first came to this land and inspired Katharine Lee Bates to write these words of what really should be our national anthem: "O beautiful for pilgrim feet / Whose stern impassioned stress / A thoroughfare for freedom beat / Across the wilderness."[1]

Those pilgrims came from a Europe that had been devastated by war and turmoil, from southern Germany where marauding armies laid waste the land and uprooted the inhabitants. When William Penn made his visit to Frankfurt, Germany, to offer land

1. Bates, "O Beautiful Spacious Skies."

PILGER RUH

in Pennsylvania, it was as though the Messiah had come to lead them to the heavenly Jerusalem. They remembered the words of Jesus, "Take my yoke upon you, and learn from me; for I am gentle and humble in heart, and you will find rest for your souls. For my yoke is easy, and my burden is light" (Matt 11:29–30).

They came seeking peace. Our English Reformed cousins settled in Massachusetts and called their village "Salem," the Hebrew word for "peace." Our German Reformed and Lutheran ancestors named their churches "Friedens," the German word for peace, and established communities named after biblical places. America was indeed the promised land where they found peace and comfort in their religious faith.

We celebrate that heritage and look back with longing to a time when religious faith meant something. Today we live in a culture that is blind to the spiritual life. The author Wayne Teasdale describes it as "spiritually illiterate, morally confused, psychologically dysfunctional, and heavily addicted to violence, entertainment, and consumerism. It is religious to a point—that is, as long as it doesn't cost too much. Most Americans, we are told, believe in God, but too few realize that life is a spiritual process."[2] It is a journey that cannot be taken for granted but must be intentional. You do not inherit your faith. You develop it.

Today there are political elements that seek to inject more religion into government but will have nothing to do with those spiritual principles upon which religion is based. We want the outward trappings of religion but not the inward life-changing spirit of religion. We want to display the Ten Commandments but not live by them. We declare ourselves a Christian nation, but we ignore the teachings of the Christ.

And yet the sociologists and poll takers tell us that there is a deep desire on the part of so many people to become more spiritual, to find the heart of God, and to gain peace for their souls. There is still that holy longing, that *Sehnsucht* of our ancestors to know and experience God on an intimate level.

2. Rohr, *Contemplation in Action*, 154.

Gray Matter, Dark Matter, and Doesn't Matter

The desire to know and experience the love of God was the goal of the German contemplatives. The Rhineland mystics such as Hildegard of Bingen and Mechteld of Magdeburg sought the journey into the heart of God, not only to find inner peace but also to be the expression of that peace and love of God to all the world. It is not enough to find rest for your soul; you must also share that peace with others. The journey into the heart of God is also the journey into the heart of the world.

Over the years there have been many attempts by socially concerned artists to call attention to the poverty, famine, and disease that affects many parts of the world and to implore the leaders of the richest nations to help end this poverty. Their slogan has been "We don't want your money; we want your voice, your prayers, your conscious awareness, your effort of will." "To do justice, and to love kindness, and to walk humbly with your God" is not only the teaching of the prophet Micah; it is the teaching of Jesus, of Buddha, of Muhammad, of Moses. To love others is to journey into the heart of God. To offer a cup of cold water to any of God's children is to journey into the heart of God.

Jonny Kennedy was a young man who died at the age of thirty-six. Jonny had a rare and painful genetic condition called dystrophic epidermolysis bullosa (EB), a condition that can cause its sufferer's skin to literally fall off. In his last months, while battling terminal skin cancer, Jonny worked with filmmaker Patrick Collerton to document his life and death.

Instead of becoming bitter and angry at the world and at God for enduring a life of agony and frustration, Kennedy maintained a courageous spirit and inner calm. Out of kindness and selflessness he shared with the world in every way that was available to him all the lessons he learned—about himself, about death, and most importantly about life. He shared himself and gave himself in the documentary film *The Boy Whose Skin Fell Off* up to his moment of death which occurred during the filming. In his dying, he found the meaning of his living and what it means to bear the yoke of pain and suffering. He was able to see through this into the love of God.

Jonny Kennedy helps us to understand that you need not be bound by the kind of world in which you live or the expectations laid upon us by the culture in which we live. Our ancestors have shown us that you can take the initiative and change the way you live. They left the past and came to this place.

We, too, can change. There is power to change. We often use the word "repent" in church. This word when used in the Gospels is most often a translation of the Greek word *metanoia* which means to "change one's mind." We are to go beyond the mind that we have been given and acquired, go beyond the mind shaped by the culture to the mind that you have "in Christ"

God created humans, but God also endowed humans to recreate, to begin again, to continue the process of becoming. Change is indeed the only constant in the universe.

Pilger Ruh was not a stopping point on the trail to peace but a place to rest and then to resume the task of creating peace in oneself and in the world.

"A FEATHER ON THE
BREATH OF GOD"

There are occasions when I have a deep desire to live in a time other than our current age. There are times when I find myself falling in love with a woman who lived hundreds of years ago. Sometimes I have memories of events that could not possibly be mine since they have occurred long before I was born. Even some of my dreams seem to defy comprehension. Are all these latent traces of previous lives that I am often frustrated in trying to remember?

When I first learned of Hildegard of Bingen there was an immediate admiration and even some familiarity. The more I tried to rediscover this woman, the more I became aware that an unprecedented number of people in our culture were also enamored of this nine-hundred-year-old mystic, considered one of the greatest geniuses of the Middle Ages.

Hildegard was a Benedictine abbess who was a theologian, composer, artist, poet, visionary, and social critic. She also preached and wrote letters of spiritual counsel to popes, kings, bishops, nuns, and educated laity, male and female, all over Europe. Hildegard was a healer, using a holistic approach by recognizing the power within the person to bring about natural healing. She wrote an informed thesis on the healing arts, incorporating her own scientific use of herbs which grew in abundance at her abbey in Rupertsburg, Germany.

Hildegard referred to herself as merely "a feather on the breath of God" in order to show that God can use any individual, even the weakest and most insignificant, as a manifestation of God's presence and glory. A small feather that is borne by the wind can fly because it is lifted up by another power, so Hildegard attributes her accomplishments to the presence of God within her.

Born in the year 1098, the tenth child in a family of minor nobility, she was dedicated to the church and sent to an anchoress, Jutta, for education. When Jutta died, Hildegard was elected abbess at the small convent at Disibodenberg. She died in 1179 at the age of 81, but what she accomplished in her years of living would satisfy several lifetimes. Hildegard was called the "Sybil on the Rhine"—the Sybil being the prophetess and mouthpiece of the gods in ancient mythology. Named a doctor of the church, she was canonized by Pope Benedict XVI on May 10, 2012, although she had been considered a saint for centuries prior.

Why has Hildegard of Bingen become the saint for our age, a woman who represents much of contemporary theology, science, creativity, social equality, and more? Consider that she was a political and social activist, writing letters to her ecclesiastical hierarchy, even the pope, advocating change. Some say that she was a forerunner of the Reformation since she denounced corruption in the church. While she did not consider herself a feminist, she certainly would be at the forefront of the feminist movement today, demanding that women should be heard. She compared herself to Judith and David in the Bible who lopped off the heads of male giants. Her views on the ancient goddess religions and her emphasis on the Virgin Mary exemplify this. Nevertheless, she was a product of her times, firmly believing that chastity was the noblest of virtues and that sexual lust was demonic.

When I consider my activism and the use of the arts and jazz in worship, early work in the environmental movement, and Celtic spirituality, with its emphasis on panentheism, I find that Hildegard personifies my own interests and pursuits. Her creative expressions, whether in music, illuminations deriving from her visions, poetry, and other writings, all reflect her belief in the wholeness of creation. All things come from God, God is in all things, and ultimately all things will be reconciled to God. In the same way, the earth itself is sacred and must not be injured or destroyed. Humans, in their physical form and psyche, are seen as manifestations of God's larger creation.

Hildegard possessed a deep love for the church which she regarded as the bride of Christ. And yet, her theology has universal appeal. You can find elements of a Native American worldview, Eastern religious thought (especially Buddhist—consider her mandalas), Celtic spirituality, and others. Her mystical theology declares that God is apprehended not only with the head but also with the heart. God is in all things.

As one who believes in the possibility of reincarnation, it is conceivable that aspects of Hildegard's spirit have been infused in other minds and have found new expression in subsequent arts, science, medicine, etc. If death is a re-merging of the individual spirit with the greater spirit of the creator, then may it also be possible that some aspect will find new birth in other humans. In the end, we are all one.

VISIONS OF ST. JOAN

The Metropolitan Museum of Art in New York City was my childhood hangout, even before my artist uncle, Emilio, moved back from Florence, Italy, to an apartment on East 84th Street. I would visit him there, as well as the studio he maintained in Florence years later. Both the Met and Emilio instilled in me a love of the arts, and I spent much of my youth visiting museums and contemplating the great works, especially that of the Renaissance painters, the Romantics, neorealists, and early impressionists.

I was very happy that the Metropolitan provided benches in the galleries. Most tourists would just rush through the halls, glancing quickly at the paintings, perhaps stopping a bit longer at famous works that they recognized. It wasn't like the lines that I had encountered in the Louvre of those waiting to see Mona Lisa.

There was one particular painting that especially intrigued me, and I would make a pilgrimage to its gallery on each visit and sit for a while in contemplation. Jules Bastien-Lepage had depicted Joan of Arc at the moment of her vision, and his painting had a transcendent quality about it. I would look into the face of Joan as she was trying to grasp the meaning of the message that she had just heard from the celestial and ghostly figures appearing in back of her.

At her trial, Joan had claimed that she had a vision of the archangel Michael bidding her to lead the armies of France against the English invaders. Joan also had visions of Margaret and Catherine, two virgin saints martyred in their teens for disobeying the church.

Joan was accused of heresy for claiming that she had received instructions from God through his intermediary, Michael. Only the church could speak for God; therefore Joan's divine instructions were illegal. The English tribunal that passed judgment did so based on her blasphemy by wearing men's clothes, acting upon visions that may have been demonic rather than angelic, and refusing to submit her words and deeds to the judgment of the church.

Visions, both words and images appearing in the minds of persons, directing them to alternate courses of action, were certainly not uncommon, especially to persons open to the spiritual realm. The apostle Peter, seeking to evade Nero's persecution of the Christians, had a vision of the Christ on the Appian Way. He asked, "*Domine, quo vadis?*" "Lord, where are you going?" And Christ answered, "I am going to Rome to be crucified again." And so the embarrassed Peter also returned to Rome and was crucified upside down, since he didn't want to die like his Lord.

Saul of Tarsus, a Roman Jew commissioned by the chief priests to hunt down Christians, was traveling on the Damascus Road when he heard a voice saying, "Saul, Saul, why are you persecuting me? It hurts you to kick against the goads." I asked, "Who are you, Lord?" The Lord answered, "I am Jesus whom you are persecuting. But get up and stand on your feet; for I have appeared to you for this purpose, to appoint you to serve and testify to the things in which you have seen me and to those in which I will appear to you. I will rescue you from your people and from the Gentiles—to whom I am sending you to open their eyes so that they may turn from darkness to light and from the power of Satan to God, so that they may receive forgiveness of sins and a place among those who are sanctified by faith in me" (Acts 26:13–18).

The pagan Roman emperor Constantine, engaged in a war against his co-emperor, Maxentius, had marched his army to the Tiber River and was facing the superior forces of his enemy. According to the historian Eusebius of Caesarea, the day before the Battle of the Milvian Bridge, Constantine had a vision of the Chi Rho, the XP, the first two letters in Greek for Christ. He heard the words, "*In hoc signo vinces*," "By this sign you will conquer." The following night, in a dream, Christ told him to place the sign on the labarum, the army standard. He did. They won. And Constantine became a Christian—although he waited until he was on his deathbed before being baptized.

Throughout the ages, men and women reported having otherworldly visions with instructions that would alter their lives and the lives of others. From the medieval Rhineland mystics such as Hildegard of Bingen to the many contemporary religions and sects where visions, speaking in tongues, and other abnormal communications occur, the eternal question is "How does one hear the voice of God?" Modern psychology most often attributes these hallucinations to a form of madness. If that is the case, then the very nature of religion is suspect since not only Jesus of Nazareth and many of his followers, but also Moses, Gautama, Mohammed, Native American shamans, and other founders of religion, were visionaries who were in direct communication with God.

In his early years, Ralph Waldo Emerson was a Unitarian pastor. The Unitarian Church evolved from Congregationalism, the religion of the pilgrims and a forerunner of the United Church of Christ. Emerson and his friend Henry David Thoreau were among the founders of the Transcendentalist movement in America. This philosophy emphasizes the individual's freedom of thought, that the divine is most comprehended within the person, rather than inherited from historic beliefs. While I find much merit in this philosophy, it seems limited to the individual's perception of reality.

When I contemplate the image of Joan of Arc, I recognize the need to be sensitive to visions of the divine, to the inner light, to the voice of God as I hear and interpret it. But at the same time, I must consider this in the context of other voices, the God who speaks in the many sounds of the world, its culture, its religions, its philosophies. Visions are not to be ignored but framed in a greater reality of a universal consciousness: that of a God who is present in all things.

KNOWING SNOW

The Eskimos have fourteen words for snow. Those who spend their lives on the sea would recognize the many shades of blue and have a greater sense of the color, turbidity, and movement of water.

A tour guide on St. Maarten in the Netherlands Antilles said that each of the tiny island's thirty-two beaches is characterized by different types of sand and that a seasoned beachcomber could look at your legs and feet and deduce which strip of oceanfront you last visited as indicated by the color and graininess of the sand.

When you spend your life in one place or are devoted to a field of study, or are obsessed with a particular subject, you see and understand with greater precision and clarity. Your environment becomes a part of you, and you become intensely aware of everything that surrounds you. Consciousness is the awareness of self and the self's interaction with its environment.

Zen Buddhism is a philosophy and art of awareness. There is a classic Zen story that illustrates this.

After ten years of apprenticeship, Tenno achieved the rank of Zen teacher. One rainy day, he went to visit the famous master Nan-in. When he walked in, the master greeted him with a question: "Did you leave your wooden clogs and umbrella on the porch?" "Yes," Tenno replied. "Tell me," the master continued, "did you place your umbrella to the left of your shoes, or to the right?" Tenno did not know the answer and realized that he had not yet attained full awareness. So he became Nan-in's apprentice and studied under him for ten more years.

The fifth-grade teacher who keeps telling her students to pay attention is practicing a form of Zen.

How can you pay attention to a single snowflake? Some physicists have calculated the weight of one flake to an infinitesimally small degree of a fraction of a milligram. In other words, one flake weighs next to nothing. Yet, as an old parable suggests, one more flake falling on a branch with four million other flakes is enough to snap the limb. The fable makes the point that it may take just one more voice to be heard to bring peace to the world. The sound of many voices, like the voice of many angels heard by the prophet John, may accomplish what it intends. So we do not hesitate to speak out when change is necessary.

The weather reporter indicated that we would have a huge accumulation of snow. I sat on my enclosed back porch and watched my yard fill up with the frozen white raindrops and thought of the various functionaries at Gobbler's Nob on Groundhog Day earlier in the month, and I wondered why they didn't put a blindfold on the groundhog before they pulled him from his hole. But that would be too much like the man who petitioned the Pennsylvania Department of Highways to move the "Deer Crossing" sign from in front of his property because he didn't want the deer to cross there.

Signs are not reality. They only point to what is important. Signs can point in different directions and still be correct. You can go to an intersection on Route 222 in Pennsylvania and find a sign pointing to the right that reads "Allentown—15 miles." Someone could also erect a sign pointing to the left which might read "Allentown—25,000 miles." Both would be correct, but one would be more useful than the other.

Each of us is on our own spiritual journey to discover the nature of God and the meaning of our own lives. There are many signs along the way indicating which path we might follow. Some may reveal a direct route to accomplish what we believe is our destiny. Others may go in another direction. In the United States we have traffic circles which are labeled "roundabouts." In the United

Kingdom they are called "diversions." And there may be more truth to that, for our lives are constantly filled with diversions, roads not taken. Like Robert Frost, taking the less traveled path may make all the difference.

Memory often tends to distort reality. The snows of yesterday, the days of early childhood, were deeper because we were different then. Did memory exaggerate the amount of snow that fell on the streets of my youth? Or did the amount simply overwhelm the smallness of a six-year-old body?

It was a winter without warmth. From early December the snow just accumulated, so that by late February the pile of snow in my backyard was more than twice my height. Since our neighboring house was vacant at the time, their yard became a community dumping ground for snow. The huge pile eventually reached to the second floor of the house. Some of the older kids got the idea of creating a massive igloo and hollowed out the gigantic mound. For several weeks, until the spring thaw, it became a gathering place for the boys and girls on our street and in the area. Within the cold of the icy room, there was the warmth of friendship and a continual reminder of relationships formed years ago that continue, some in memory and a few in occasional contact.

The indigenous peoples of North America spoke of the Snow Moon, the full moon that appeared in February, often a time when there was much snow on the ground. It was also called the Hunger Moon, for the snow made it difficult to forage for food. But it was not without hope, for underneath, life was beginning to stir. The February Snow Moon was a time for hoping and remembering.

December is also a time to remember. The popularity of the 1960 musical *The Fantastiks* has to do in part with remembering. Indeed, its first song is the beautiful ballad, "Try to Remember," encouraging one to recall past experiences both bitter and sweet.

The Belgian playwright Maurice Maeterlinck tells of meeting an old woman in a garden who describes in the most vivid detail all of the flowers, their colors and shapes, and how they interact with each other. Only later did he discover that she was blind. He asked her how she was able to describe the contents of the garden to such perfection when she was unable to see. She answered that it was from memory—from the time in life when she could see and took the time to look at the beauties of nature as if she would never see them again.

In the twilight of our years, deep in December when all we will have left is memory, it would be well if those memories were good ones. The years pass, the snows are gone, but we can remember the flowers. We can let the memory of things past be the prologue for what is to come—in this life and the next.

FAILURE TO COMMUNICATE

Kaang is a language spoken by about thirty-five thousand people in a part of Burma. The leader of the people is a guru, a word derived from the Sanskrit meaning a mentor or teacher. So the "Kaang guru" is a tribal teacher and leader. I don't know if somehow this word and its meaning migrated to Australia and became the name for the animal that hops from place to place.

There is a local myth in Australia that relates a story of when an early explorer, Lt. James Cook, first saw this strange marsupial, he asked a local tribesman what it was. The Aborigine replied, "kanguru," which in his language meant, "I don't know."

Aboriginal Australians are said to have migrated from southeast Asia during the Pleistocene era, so perhaps elements of their original tongue migrated with them. Language itself evolves in strange ways as those who use it migrate and evolve. Common descriptive words can take on derisive overtones and become offensive. I doubt if kangaroos are upset at what we call them, but Aboriginal Australians don't like the term "aborigine."

"Aborigine" seems to come from the Latin meaning, "from the original," and originally referred to the early residents of southern Italy who came from Greece. Everybody is originally from somewhere else. The human race is migratory, and so we are all immigrants.

The languages we use are also migratory. We don't know where and how they have originated. One of the most famous lines in cinematic history is from *Cool Hand Luke* when Captain says to Luke, "What we've got here is a failure to communicate." We want to understand and we want to be understood. This goes back thousands of years to primitive humans. Recently, scientists have discovered proto-humans making symbols on the walls of a cave that pre-date the Chauvet and Lascaux pictographs in France that go back thirty-five thousand years. Humans, like other life forms, may have an inherent desire to communicate. Several philologists, including Max Muller, advanced the so-called "bow-wow" or "cuckoo" theory, speculating that our early ancestors first tried imitating the sounds of animals, birds, or other natural sounds and rhythms. This onomatopoetic theory was largely discredited.

While attending Lancaster Theological Seminary, a bishop from the Church of South Africa, Clifford Kuzwayo, was also a student. His wife spoke one of the six hundred Bantu languages, either Sandawe or Hadza. We often asked her to speak in her native tongue because its unique feature was a dental clicking sound for consonants. It was a language that was unfamiliar to us.

Mary Ann's family spoke Hungarian. While I might be able to get by in the Germanic and Romance languages that have many derivatives in English, Hungarian originated in Siberia and borrowed words from the Turkish and Persian languages. It is one of the most difficult languages for Westerners to learn.

Our attempts to communicate have advanced almost to the point of regression. As a preacher, I have viewed my role to interpret the Scriptures, words written two thousand years ago, for a modern audience. I have tried to tell people that the gospel hasn't changed, but the packaging needs to. Language—communication—is really exegesis or interpretation.

And yet, in this age of multitasking, I have looked down from the pulpit to see many young people, and even some adults, listening to and scanning their phones. When I asked some of my teens what they were doing, one replied that he was listening to the broadcast version of the sermon through his earbuds. Another said that he was just checking ChatGPT to see if my sermon was a product of artificial intelligence. Is modern technology enhancing the failure to communicate or simply testing the veracity of it?

Gray Matter, Dark Matter, and Doesn't Matter

My grandmother Natalie Wertz, with whom we lived when I was a child, was fluent in seven languages: German, Russian, Polish, Ukrainian, Dutch, English, and Farsi. While English and German were the dominant languages spoken in our house, other foreign words crept into the conversation and we quickly had to interpret them based upon the context. Farsi was not spoken at all since this was the language that Natalie had used as a child in her native Russia to communicate with her Persian servants. It was a reminder of her upper middle-class roots in Tsaritsyn before she gave up her somewhat luxurious lifestyle and became a hausfrau in the German-speaking neighborhood of "down-neck" Newark, New Jersey. Although, had she remained in her homeland, the Russian Revolution would have deprived her of her status and sent her, along with her Volga-German relatives, into exile in Kazakhstan and Siberia.

One of my great regrets, now that I am in my older years, is that I didn't listen to all of her stories, write them down, and encouraged her to remember and tell more. Teenagers are existentialists. They live in the now and are not interested in the past. It was indeed a failure to communicate. How many stories are lost because of our refusal to listen? That is why I encourage people to record their meaningful life events—for themselves and for others. Our stories shape our lives, and they may have a profound effect upon the lives of others. We should not fail to communicate them.

ARS GRATIA ARTIS

Karl H. Pribram, a neuroscientist and professor at Stanford University, along with David Bohm, a theoretical physicist, and other physicists who study quantum mechanics, explored the idea that the universe is one great hologram and that one of our thought processes is to think in images. The science and psychology of consciousness is so very complex that many books have been written about it. (I have at least thirty-six books on the subject.)

We often think in images and our minds are very adept at creating symbols to represent concepts, emotions, aspirations, spirituality, and more. John Curtis Gowan refers to this as "parataxic totemization,"[1] the mind's ability to create visual symbols. Every living creature is an artist. We think in images and we create other forms to represent what is within us, whether it is painting, music, dance, and so on.

As pastor of St. John's United Church of Christ in Kutztown, Pennsylvania, I encouraged the arts in many innovative ways as a means of helping persons explore and express their own spirituality and to share their lives through artistic expression. One of the groups that used our space was the New Arts Program (NAP), founded by James Carroll, a professor in the art department at Kutztown University and a member of St. John's. I serve on its board of directors.

The New Arts Program is at the cutting edge of the arts scene and embodies the essence of what was once called "avant-garde,"

1. Gowan, *Trance, Art and Creativity*, 224.

innovative styles that stretch the mind. Performing at St. John's were artists such as Philip Glass, who came to Kutztown every four years; Allen Ginsberg; Steve Reich; John Cage; Meredith Monk, and other well-known and not-so-known artists and composers. Keith Haring, the internationally celebrated graffiti artist who grew up at St. John's, contributed his work to the church and to the New Arts Program.

Most of the works displayed by NAP are what many would call abstract. Makoto Fujimura, founder of the International Arts Movement, a bridge between the arts community and the church, prefers to use the term "essence of reality." He says, "I want my work to be a stripping off the unnecessary while it accentuates the physicality of Creation's textures, colors and materials."[2] He wants his art to be a means of experiencing reality.

"We see life not as it is but as we are."[3] Life is exegesis. Life is interpretation. What happens to us, what we see, what we hear, as well as people who are part of our lives and who contribute to our life's meaning, make us who we are and affect how we understand life.

Art is like a sermon. What the preacher may say from the pulpit may not be what the person in the pew hears. People come to the church with their own agendas and the words they hear are the words they may need or want to hear. The artist creates out of his or her own mind, and the viewer derives meaning according to his or her own frame of reference.

When I was a young boy, I often attended church by myself after Sunday school. Sitting alone in the pew at St. Stephan's Evangelical and Reformed Church, I was seldom involved in the pastor's sermons. While the earlier service was conducted in the High German language and the sermon was preached in a haranguing style that reminded one of the Third Reich (this was shortly after the end of World War II), the same sermon rendered in English at the later service was still beyond my comprehension and sometimes scary. I

2. Bustard, *It Was Good*, 298.

3. This quote is attributed to Anaïs Nin and to the Babylonian Talmud, among other sources.

was left to occupy my time in the presence of God by looking at the stained-glass windows, the paintings on the wall next to the apse depicting the martyrdom of Saint Stephan and the ascension of Christ. The artwork took me to another dimension where I could communicate with God in a different way. I would also accompany my Catholic friends to the many Roman Catholic churches in the area. There were the ethnic churches: Mount Carmel for the Italians, St. Benedict for the Germans, St. Aloysius for the Irish, Our Lady of Fatima for the Spanish, and the diocesan church, St. James. Each church had its magnificent windows, frescos, and statuary that helped the worshiper contemplate the divine.

I didn't realize it at the time, but I was practicing a form of *visio divina*, a meditative technique of contemplating a work of art, placing yourself within the painting and interacting with the environment of the artistic creation. This may be why art was such an integral part of worship through the centuries, aiding us in entering into the presence of God.

A traveling exhibition once came to the Reading area. The display was entitled *100 Artists See God*. As I walked through the gallery I saw very few works that could be considered religious in nature. There were abstract designs, pictures of dogs and mothers, a medicine cabinet, a crucified frog, a telescope, a hamburger with a Buddha in it and the caption "Make Me One With Everything." The artists were depicting that which was important to them, the secular gods they worshiped, their sarcastic observation of a society that has secularized the deity. Anais's words came back to me: "We see God, not as God is, but as we are."

Florence, Italy, is the birthplace of Renaissance art. If you want to see a representation of the masters, they are all here. My uncle Emilio, an accomplished artist, maintained a studio in the city. His work is in the realistic style, and many of his paintings are of Tuscan locales. I had the opportunity to spend some time in the city, and since I lived just over the Ponte Vecchio and within walking distance of the Uffizi Gallery, I would often sit in one of the rooms contemplating the works of Michelangelo, Da Vinci, Raphael, Botticelli, and others. Thanks to the patronage of the church, most of these artists were able to prosper and create a legacy that has blessed us centuries later. Art and religion have formed an everlasting union.

Art in all of its forms has always been a means of approaching and understanding God, for God is first of all a creator, and we are able to know God through God's creation and incarnation. This is probably the main reason that I was attracted to become pastor of St. John's. Out of a congregation of six hundred members, about forty were professionally involved in the arts, and many others exhibited creativity in a variety of forms.

For example, our music director was Dr. Frank Siekmann, an internationally known composer and former head of the music department at Kutztown University. Arthur Sinclair, a professor of speech and theater, and his wife Gail, an actress, aided in the presentation of chancel dramas in which the congregation became involved. Marilyn Buchman, who ran a dance studio, along with Joanne Carroll, a former professional dancer trained in ballet, orchestrated liturgical dances with a corps of other dancers. We invited a klezmer group who performed Israeli dances around the altar, a Russian children's group who danced to the sound of the balalaika, and others. Nancy Lounsbury incorporated signing for the deaf into liturgical dance and on one occasion performed with the University Brass Ensemble in dance, sign, dramatic reading by a special chorus to Hindemith's *Symphonic Variations on a Theme by Weber*.

The church sought to explore a variety of spiritual expressions through the music of other cultures and religions: Indonesian gamelan, Costa Rican trombones, Russian music, Israeli music, American country, Africa's Thula Sizwe, Black gospel, and more. By participating in the artistic expressions of other ethnicities, the congregation gained an appreciation for their spirituality and also expanded their own.

The Resident Clowns were especially active, not only performing occasionally during and after worship but visiting other churches. They used humor and mime to interpret the Scriptures in a tradition that goes back to the Middle Ages.

Sunday evenings focused on the arts. The first Sunday of the month was Art Cinema, where we would go to the movie theater around the corner, view a film, and return to the church for discussion. Paul Angstadt, a former mayor of Reading who owned the Strand Theater, would often book art films at my request.

The second Sunday was Left Bank, inspired by my stay on *Rive Gauche* at the Hotel Paris Latin during my student days and visits to Shakespeare and Company where some of my favorite authors of the Lost Generation—Hemingway, Fitzgerald, Eliot— would gather to discuss a variety of issues of which many found their way into their novels. In our Left Bank sessions, we talked about many things and how they influenced our spiritual lives.

The third Sunday was Spiritual Exploration. We invited leaders of other religions and no religion to share their philosophies and dogmas and how they came to travel their spiritual paths. After I had left St. John's, I continued this with the Spiritual Exploration Project, consisting of Spirit on Tap that meets in the DoubleTree Hotel, Reading, to engage in theological discussion, explore alternate views, and stimulate dialogue around issues of faith, spirituality, and current social issues; Soul Café, an informal setting for individual presentations on matters of interest and concern; Contemplative Spirituality for topics relating to personal spiritual development, individual faith journeys, and resources to improve the life of the spirit; and an annual Community Forum on relevant social issues.

The fourth Sunday was the Poetic Image, with poets reading and discussing their work and encouraging others to think poetically.

The arts were important to the congregation of St. John's. Its new wing, built in 1961, was endowed with magnificent acoustics that encouraged many orchestras, choral ensembles, jazz groups, and others to hold their performances there. We renovated the old part of the church that had been the nave and balcony of the 1876 building into a performance space with theatrical lighting, moveable acoustic partitions, and a stage which was also on rollers. The space was used not only for church productions but for community groups such as the East Penn Emerging Artists Program. Yoga and Tai Chi classes were also held here. An annual art exhibition featuring the paintings, sculpture, photography of church members was held in the very ample narthex area.

The church also published a monthly "State of the Arts" newsletter with articles about art events within the congregation, the community, and the university.

Because of its lively church programs, community involvement, and other features, at least five men and women were encouraged to enter the Christian ministry. Others excelled in the arts field, such as Debbie Walker, a Broadway dancer; Christianne Knauer Roll, daughter of Cindy Knauer, a voice teacher on our music staff, who became associate professor of musical theatre and musical theater program coordinator at Florida Southern College; Michael Brolly, noted wood sculptor of fantastic and often weird images; and Mark Amey, hand-thrown potter of exquisite design.

My son Matthew Serio had served as director of creative opportunities for the Pennsylvania Council on the Arts (PCA) handling a grants portfolio of over $6.4 million and before that was program manager with the Berks Arts Council and festival director of the Greater Reading Film Festival. He now has his own creative design company, ArtiglianoSerio.

Jungian psychology has taught us that we really think in images, not words. Whenever we have dreams, it's all in symbols. We file our thoughts in hologrammatic images rather than linear words. So when we communicate, we have to translate the images into words, speak them, send them to another's receptors, and then they are decoded into images that are meaningful. What happens very often is a breakdown in communication.

Susan L. Pena, in an article appearing in the *Reading Eagle*, "At Kutztown Church Art, Religion Reunite," quoted me:

> When we are dealing with symbols in art, it's almost a pure form. There is some translation, but it's more direct. If this is applied to scripture to explain why we have art or performance in worship, I would point out that in the Bible the prophets often used symbols. Jeremiah often

walked around Jerusalem with an ox yoke. He didn't say a word, but the symbolic gesture was important. David danced before the Lord when the Ark was brought in. There are many elements of performance that go back to scriptures.

In our Protestant culture we have learned that the verbal form is the one we ought to use, so most Protestant worship tends to be verbal prayer, reading Scriptures, the sermon, with little of anything else except music. (It must be noted, however, that in most non-Western cultures, dance and drama are inseparable from religious rites; secular art forms are almost non-existent).

In our present time, people are less likely to accept mystical experiences because we live in a materialistic, technological culture. Ever since Thomas Aquinas, we have lived with an Aristotelian kind of logic that everything has a cause and effect. When something happens, we don't ask, "What does it mean?" but rather "What caused it to happen?" In the Platonic worldview during Jesus' time, no one would have asked how he did the miracles. Instead, they would ask what it meant that he could heal people. We live with mystical experiences all around us, but we don't recognize them as such.

The various art forms that we included in the worship services at St. John's were not designed to entertain, although for some that was the result, but to enhance the experience of the worshiper by the addition of symbols that speak to the deeper levels of consciousness. God, the creator, has given us the ability to create in the same way in which God creates. It is the ability to take ideas and put them into a medium that can communicate.

The motion picture corporation Metro-Goldwyn-Mayer adopted the motto *ars gratia artis*, meaning "art for art's sake." The implication is that true art should not be used for any other purpose, such as advancing any commercial, political, or social agenda. This is somewhat ironic since MGM is in the business of making money from its pictures. One could also argue that religious artists and performers who sold their work were also acting contrary to the meaning of the phrase.

Gray Matter, Dark Matter, and Doesn't Matter

However, when art acts to inspire, communicate, express the depths of one's consciousness as in prayer, it is fulfilling its intention, and therefore it is a very necessary component of the church's mission and purpose to celebrate the glory of God in the lives of God's people.

CREATING THE
ARCHITECTURE OF A
SPIRITUAL PATH

I was apprehensive when Allen Ginsberg was scheduled to read his poetry in St. John's Church in Kutztown, Pennsylvania. His countercultural rants in his aptly named classic "Howl" spoke of a lost battalion of spiritual seekers looking for jazz or sex or soup. I thought that my congregation, as we addressed this yearning in postmodern American culture, could provide the jazz and the soup; the sex would be problematic.

As Allen sat in my study, along with Philip Glass, who had been coming to St. John's every third year to benefit the New Arts Program on whose board I served, I remembered my earlier years when Manhattan was my playground. Though many years older than I, we both had come from Newark, were familiar with the venues around Washington Square and East Village, and we both engaged in the search for Dharma and Zen. I remembered Allen's "Howl" and the obscenity trials that his poetry had generated.

And now this gay socialist poet and icon of the Beat Generation was about to stand before the altar of an old traditional Pennsylvania Dutch congregation and offer his own anacreontic verse. I whispered a silent prayer that none of our older church elders would come out this night out of curiosity to hear this celebrated nonconformist bard. I had worked to plant the seeds of a new congregation in the midst of the old, but perhaps this was going a bit too far.

While waiting for the program to begin, I asked Phillip why a growing number of Jews, including Allen, had become Buddhists. Phillip laughed and said that they were called "BU-JUs." They had embraced Buddhism in a quest for a new spirituality that wasn't tied to theism and old traditions. We didn't have the time to get into a lengthy discussion, but we touched on the common understanding of suffering. The first noble truth of Buddhism is that life is suffering, and certainly the Jewish people have experienced that from the diaspora to the pogroms to the Holocaust. It became evident that all people seek a spiritual path out of their own context. While the great theological question of the nineteenth century was "What must I do to be saved?" the great question of the twenty-first century is "What must I do to be relevant?" Or to paraphrase Viktor Frankl, "If you can find meaning in your life, you can endure anything." That search for meaning and relevance influenced how I would try to minister to others and help them along their own spiritual path.

If my own journey was diverse, it seemed plausible that it might also be for others as well. Going to the Billy Graham meetings at the old Madison Square Garden; hanging out at jazz joints in the Village; learning meditation from Lobsang Samden, the brother of the Dalai Lama, a classmate at Ursinus; exploring the mysticism of Quaker silence and the unworldly worship of the Swedenborgians; and seeking my own dwelling place for wonder and union with the creator—it was as though I had gone through a spiritual deli and selected that which I felt I needed. The one thing that was lacking was the context or matrix. And that became my theology of the incarnation: God present not only in the person of Jesus of Nazareth but in all persons. While Christ became the clearest example of "God with us," I recognize the validity of other paths where the presence of God becomes clear.

Allen Ginsberg told the story of his visit to an ashram in Oakland. He entered the room where he was to meditate, but he carried with him a notepad upon which he would write down whatever thoughts might come to him during his period of keno-sis. But the monk who admitted him took away his pad and said, "No thinking. No writing." To empty oneself one must resist intellectual constructs and simply become aware.

Our apprehension of God is often too cerebral, too intellectual. While it is true, as Johannes Kepler said, "I think Thy thoughts after Thee, O God," there also needs to be room for the experiential. And that was what we sought to provide at St. John's.

My ministry recognized the evolutionary nature of consciousness as one develops his or her own spirituality. Using the arts as a means of expression, as well as discussion, intellectual stimulation, infusion of ideas not normally entertained, and musical forms that resonate at different levels, we sought to help persons explore their own levels of spiritual development.

Ulrich Zwingli, one of the fathers of the Reformed tradition, had another perspective, perhaps more suited to his times. Fearing the misinterpretation of images and the use of music, he whitewashed the frescoes and murals in the Grossmunster in Zurich, knocked out the stained-glass windows, and took an ax to the great organ, claiming that these additions to worship might distort the interpretation of the Gospel. Since the Bible stated that faith comes from "hearing" the word of God (Rom 10:17), only the reading of the Scriptures and preaching were important. Art and music were distractions.

The United Church of Christ has adopted the motto "God is still speaking," and we understand that to mean that God speaks in many diverse ways and with many voices. Faith comes from listening to each other in community, and people have different ways of expressing their feelings about their faith. Some use the visual arts or drama or music to express what is in their souls. Indeed, the jazz idiom began as the soulful expression of field slaves longing for freedom and looking to God for salvation.

Art is meditation. Music is the sound of the universe. Dance is the rhythm of the soul. These are all means of expressing one's spirituality. Of course there are other means of expression, but the use of the arts became the means of reaching persons who wanted to express what was inside of them and to learn from others on similar spiritual quests.

In the course of my thirty-two-year ministry at the church, our worship styles were eclectic: services of meditation using the resonating sounds of Tibetan prayer bowls; the annual Celtic service with the Shanachians, a *ceilidh* group; the African rhythms of Thula Sizwe; the haunting mysticism of the Russian Orthodox liturgy; the klezmer sounds of Sephardic Judaism and circle dances around the Lord's Table; and of course jazz. As a founder of the Berks Jazz Fest and long-time festival chairman, I introduced jazz worship services, including a Dixieland service on All Saints Sunday.

Our exploration of diverse spiritual styles was not confined to Sunday worship but also found expression in the arts and alternative healing ministries. We offered classes in yoga, Feldenkreis, and tai chi and held regular reiki and jyorei sessions, often after worship. Keith Haring, the internationally-known graffiti artist who died of AIDS, was a member of the church. He gave us a sizeable donation which became an endowment for the arts. Since roughly 8 percent of the congregation were either professionally employed in the arts, were performers or teachers, or received training in music, dance, and the other arts, it was only natural to use their talents to help them or others explore their spirituality through creative expression. A Stanislavsky class in method acting led to chancel dramas. Liturgical dance and even Christian clowning were part of the program. With five part-time musicians on the staff, three choirs, an orchestra, and various ensembles, the congregation attracted people through music and the arts, but they soon found that their quest for relevant spiritual expression was being met in other ways.

A weekly "Soul Café" explored spirituality in film, discussed contemporary events and social justice issues, explored divergent paths to expressing one's faith, and used open poetry sessions, called "The Poetic Image," to foster creativity and discussion. Using grants from the Pennsylvania Council for the Arts and the Haring Endowment, we also had "Soul Cabaret," a series of international performing groups ranging from the Indonesian gamelan to Costa Rican trombones to the Russian balalaika with a children's dance and choral group.

The essence of what we sought to accomplish was to create an open and diverse environment for worship and spiritual expression where persons could encounter a God who was speaking to them in a language they could understand. In the course of my ministry we welcomed into our fellowship persons who were raised as Mennonites, Jews, Catholics, and even Methodists, as well as persons who remained practicing Buddhists, Wiccans, Quakers, and others.

The church of my youth was destroyed in the Martian invasion that took place in the early years of the twenty-first century. Its steeple came crashing down into Ferry Street in Newark, New Jersey, when the aliens surfaced from beneath the street, as frightened residents scattered before the onslaught of the deadly rays. Steven Spielberg had used St. Stephan's United Church of Christ as his headquarters while filming *War of the Worlds*. While much of the destruction was computer generated, it was nevertheless disconcerting to see my church destroyed by an alien invasion. It was symbolic of many inner-city congregations that had failed to become relevant to a changing neighborhood and different spiritual expression. It transitioned from a congregation that numbered over three thousand the year I was baptized to less than seven when it finally ceded its ministry to another denomination and to another age.

In other writings, I had referred to St. Stephan's as the "Church of the Vanishing Jesus." One of the unusual features of the church was its large ornate enclosed pulpit. Its central and elevated position above the altar emphasized the importance of the sermon in worship. Since "faith comes from what is heard, and what is heard comes through the word of Christ" (Rom 10:17), preaching was dominant in its tradition.

To make sure that it was the word of the Lord that was emanating from the pulpit, there was a large statue of Christ, with hands outstretched, and mounted on a pedestal affixed to the rear panel of the pulpit. The panel was on a pivot which could be turned when the preacher entered the pulpit. Most likely the intended theology was that the preacher stands in the place of Christ and speaks for Christ when delivering the sermon. The reality was that Jesus leaves when the pastor appears, or that he turns his back on what is being said about him.

Matthew Theis was the first minister to come to St. Stephan's from the Reformed side of the merger with the Evangelical Synod of North America, being steeped in the Mercersburg theology as taught at Lancaster Theological Seminary. He was horrified at the thought of being Jesus' "supply" or substitute preacher, so he refused to ask Jesus to leave. It was better, he maintained, to have Jesus in back of him, bestowing his blessing upon the pastor's words.

Matt Theis was a large man, looking every bit like images of Martin Luther, and like Luther, he loved his beer. One Sunday morning he mounted the pulpit to stand in front of Jesus, but the two of them could not fit in the same space, and Matt accidentally broke the arms of the statue. The plaster Jesus was removed from the panel, and the next week Pastor Theis's sermon was "Christ Has No Hands but Our Hands."

Jesus has been restored to his rightful place above the altar, but most of the recent pastors have chosen to preach from the lectern rather than ask Christ to leave.

I had never had a problem with the theology of the vanishing Jesus. Mercersburg emphasized the sacrament of Holy Communion as the outward and visible sign of the presence of Christ among us and the primary focus of the church's worship. The incarnation was a central ingredient of the faith, for not only was God manifest in Jesus of Nazareth, but God is still present and speaking in the world today. Matt Theis was right: Jesus does not leave us but is in us as we live out the Christlike life. Nevertheless, while I don't require the presence of a statue to remind me of that, somehow the departure of the physical Jesus emphasized the continuing work of the Holy Spirit through his disciples. Today, we must be the Christ to others, and recognize the Christ-Spirit in others and help them become aware of the God that dwells within them.

In my valedictory to the congregation of St. John's, I reminded them that the only constant in the universe is change and that the first word of Jesus at the start of his ministry was *metanoia*— "change your mind." To be relevant to those who still hunger for spiritual direction, the church must constantly seek to adapt the gospel to a new age. God is still speaking, but it is the translation that will be important.

"TELL ME YOUR NAME"

Whenever my father would see me alone with my books, he would ask me what I was reading and then begin to question me about it. Our ninth-grade English semester was focused on Graeco-Roman and Norse mythology and was a particular favorite of mine.

Dad stopped by and asked me the question, "Who is Nobody?" I waited for the punchline to this apparent riddle, but he just told me to look it up. I hadn't gotten that far in reading Homer's *Odyssey*, but there is the story of Odysseus' confrontation with the cyclops Polyphemus.

When Odysseus stops at Polyphemus's island to reprovision for his voyage home, the one-eyed son of the sea-god Poseidon devours two of the sailors. He later snacks on two more for breakfast and another two for dinner. Odysseus manages to get Polyphemus drunk and the giant says to him, "Tell me your name and I will eat you last." Odysseus says that his name is *Outis*, which is Greek for "Nobody."

After Polyphemus falls into a drunken stupor, Odysseus drives a burning stake into his eye, blinding him. The cyclops yells out in pain to his fellow giants, and they ask him who is hurting him. Polyphemus replies, "Nobody is hurting me," so his brothers ignore him. Odysseus and his men manage to escape the island of the Cyclopes and sail off on their journey home.

Knowing a person's name has several implications. To know the name is to know the person. Since Polyphemus violated the ancient laws of hospitality and had some of the crew for dinner, his blinding was interpreted as punishment for this breach of etiquette.

In ancient Hebrew culture, knowing a person's name was regarded as having some control over that person. In Genesis God gives man management responsibility over all of earth's creatures (Gen 2:20) by telling him to name all the birds and beasts. In this version of the creation story man is the steward of the earth, God's caretaker.

There is also the story of Jacob wrestling with the angel (Gen 32:24–30), who in addition is referred to as God. Jacob asks, "Tell, me, I pray, your name," which God refuses since it was believed that the essence of a person was concentrated in his name. On the other hand, God changes Jacob's name to "Israel," which means "God prevails." Other interpretations suggest that God is the object and therefore it means one who has "struggled with God."

We all have our encounters with God as we wrestle with the meaning of our own existence and the question of whether there is a God who has created and is in control of the universe. Jacob's wrestling may have been with his own fears and doubts—and his desire to know the purpose of his life.

Later on in the Bible, it was Moses, wandering in the wilderness of his own despair, having been exiled from his people in Egypt, who saw a burning bush on Horeb. God speaks to Moses and asks him to deliver the people of Israel from their suffering in Egypt. Moses then says to God, "But the people will ask who has sent him. They want to know your name." God's reply is "I am who I am. Tell the people 'I am' has sent me to you" (Exod 3:14). It is interesting that the name of God is not so much a noun but a verb. God's name, rendered as Yahweh (or YHWH), is simply a form of "to be." God "is."

Names are powerful, and they have implications far beyond the individual person. It's always a mystery how parents choose the names for their children. While many select names that sound nice or connote a form of elegance, some are named for family members or have ethnic significance.

Gray Matter, Dark Matter, and Doesn't Matter

I was named after my father, but the meaning of my name, Harry, just doesn't seem appropriate for my calling. "Harry" is derived from the Germanic term "home ruler," or from the Norse "warrior king." It's not a name I would have chosen.

When selecting the names for my own children, it was just as arbitrary. My first-born son was named for my interest in Celtic spirituality studies in Scotland. My daughter bears the name of my German grandmother who emigrated from Russia. She also has as a middle name the Greek word for truth, "aletheia." My youngest son was named for the pericope readings from the Bible appointed to be read on Good Friday, the day he was born. I'm sure that he is grateful that they weren't Habakkuk or Obadiah.

People, of course, do change their names. In Hollywood, it was customary to change the names of actors and actresses so that they would look good on marquees, posters, or other publicity. Some were changed to avoid ethnic-sounding names such as Cherilyn Sarkisian who is known simply as Cher or Emanuel Goldenberg who became Edward G. Robinson. Archibald Leach wasn't romantic enough, so his name became Cary Grant. British actor Stewart Granger had to change his name because his original name, James Stewart, was used by an actor from Pennsylvania. Famous authors have adopted pen names as well

Native Americans may have had the right idea. A child was given a name at birth, but during adolescence, the young man went on a "vision quest" which may have included time in a sweat lodge. During this time he would have a vision of what his name really should be. For example, the Lakota war chief, when he was a boy, got into a fight, and his face was splattered like rain with the blood of his adversary. He became known as Chief Rain-in-the-Face and fought against Custer at the Battle of the Little Big Horn. Coincidentally, his adopted name was reinforced when he also fought a battle during a heavy downpour.

Names are important to commemorate all who have lived on this earth. We place their names on tombstones, memorial plaques, cenotaphs, and other ways to remind us of their presence. This is especially true of those who have fallen in battle or perished at sea. Woody Guthrie wrote a song about the hundred sailors who died when the USS Reuben James was the first naval vessel to be sunk by Nazi U-boats at the start of World War II. Their names, like thousands of others who died in service to their country, are remembered in song and story, in monuments, and in the hearts of their loved ones.

In the Jewish religion, remembering the dead enables them to live on in memory. Most synagogues have a *yahrzeit* wall with the names of members who have died and a light that is lit on the yearly anniversary of their death. At Yad Vashem, the Holocaust memorial in Jerusalem, the names of murdered Jews are recorded in the Hall of Names so that they will not be forgotten.

The great question is that of the afterlife and how our identities will be preserved—if they are. Will we retain our names? For those who believe in reincarnation, what is their "soul name," since each incarnation would have its own identity? Are we known by the collective names of each person we are on the earth?

In this world, there are many ways in which people worship God. Indeed, God is worshiped by many names, literally hundreds of them, depending upon how God is manifest to the believer. But in the end, God simply is, as we will be when we are assumed into the spirit that created us.

HOMEWORK

There is always something missing in our lives. We spend so much of our time looking for things that are misplaced. Saint Anthony must be quite busy looking for cell phones, car keys, books, and other items. As children we learned the prayer, "Saint Anthony, Saint Anthony, please come around. Something is lost and needs to be found." The saint has proven helpful, for eventually, our subconscious mind remembered where we had lost the object of our quest.

Humans are always looking for that which is lost. Whether it's the holy grail, the ark of the covenant, pirate treasure, or lost kingdoms, we seem to be on an endless quest. We seem to be on a lifelong search for that which will bring happiness, peace, and fulfillment to our lives.

The birth narratives of Jesus of Nazareth contain several searches: Joseph and Mary's search for a room at an inn; the magi's search for a king; the shepherd's search for a messiah; King Herod's search to destroy a rival to his power; Jesus' parents' search for a place of refuge in a distant land. And later in his life, many would come to the disciple Philip saying, "Sir, we wish to see Jesus." The Gospels represent the human search for the spiritual dimension of our lives. Ever since Adam and Eve were banished from Eden, their descendants have always had an inner longing to return to the place of their beginning, to where they have always felt they belong—to the womb of their origin.

Viktor Frankl said in his book *Man's Search for Meaning* that it was our need for relevance and purpose that enables us to continue the journey through life. Native Americans prescribed a rite of passage for their children that begins in the sweat lodge and continues with the vision quest and encounters with their spirit guides in order to identify who they are and what their path through life should be.

Whether it is the innate desire for meaning, relevance, purpose, or identity, what we are really seeking is a place to which we belong, a place called home, a place to feel safe and secure.

When African Americans sought to escape from the scourge of slavery, they expressed their hopes and dreams through their spiritual songs, many of which used "home" as their heartfelt longing. For example, "Steal away, steal away home," "Trampin', trampin', trying to make heaven my home," "Swing low, sweet chariot, coming for to carry me home," "Sometimes I feel like a motherless child, a long way from home."

In my life, there have been many places where I have lived. Each one was home, a place of formation, growth, and nourishing. When I was born, Mom and Dad rented a small second-floor apartment above a shoe store on Wilson Avenue in Newark, New Jersey's Ironbound section. Here I began my life of exploration by crawling out a window onto a garage roof before being rescued by my mother when I got too close to the edge.

My second home was a first-floor flat around the corner on Marne Street. There were only four rooms, but I had a room all to myself with no furnishings except a crib which was on wheels. Here I learned to throw my weight around by running into the inside headboard which propelled my bed across the floor so I could see what was going on. Aunt Dotty lived with us while her new husband, Frank, was off fighting in the Pacific. Number thirteen Marne Street was also home to my father's many boxing friends who would gather to watch the Saturday night fights on our fourteen-inch console television.

I was in my pre-teens when we moved to Monroe Street in a different neighborhood. A real sense of home developed in the few years that we lived there. My father brought home a dog which sort of took his place since he was seldom around. I began my career in the news delivery business with my first paper route. And I thought I was heading for a different career in astronomy or in chemistry. The basement of the two-family apartment building provided space for my laboratory where I accumulated a variety of chemicals, including charcoal, sulfur, and potassium nitrate, so I could blow things up in the backyard.

With my parents' divorce and my grandfather's death, we moved back to Marne Street and the Wertz homestead, which ended up being in the family for more than a hundred years. Mom went to work for Bell Labs and Western Electric while grandmother Natalie raised my brothers and me. The small four-room house with a basement kitchen was the gathering place for our extended family. It still wonders me (to use a Pennsylvania-Dutch expression) how fourteen people plus occasional guests could fit around a dining room table in an 18 x 14-foot room. When I recall our holiday celebrations with delicacies from the city's specialty shops—German, Jewish, Italian, Polish, Russian—and the joyous, fun-loving conversations, it was indeed the happiest of occasions. We were together; we belonged to each other; we were family; we were loved. It was home.

Home is where your heart is. Home is where you know and are known. Home is where you feel safe. Home is also memory, a place to which you cannot return because the time and place no longer exist, except in the mind. And yet, it is that sense of home that compels us to continue our journey through life to the fulfillment of all our hopes and aspirations. Home is within the heart of God, not a physical location but being present in the heart of God and being aware of God's grace and love.

"Once Jesus was asked by the Pharisees when the kingdom of God was coming, and he answered, 'The kingdom of God is not coming with things that can be observed; nor will they say, "Look, here it is!" or "There it is!" For, in fact, the kingdom of God is among you'" (Luke 17:20–21).

Heaven, or home, or the kingdom is within each of us. Our only real work in this life is homework, the work that brings you home.

UNCLE PEPPERS

My grandfather Luigi Serio had ten children, two by his first wife. When she died, Luigi returned to Italy, married her sister, and had eight more children. It was a most peculiar set of siblings, for among them were an artist, a boxer, a would-be nun, a junkyard entrepreneur, a talented baker, a Broadway aficionado, a bookie, and a restaurateur. They were all colorful characters who knew how to entertain one another at their weekly post-prandial sessions on Sunday.

Gene was the music lover and instigator of many of the pranks and jokes that the Serios were known for. He was also renowned among family members for his pecuniary interests and somewhat parsimonious ways. Uncle Gene always kept a small notebook in his pocket and recorded every expenditure from his hamburger lunch to his bar tab, even if it was only one drink. If he found a dime in the street, it was duly noted in his book.

Gene had a heart condition and went to see a cardiologist. After his visit with the doctor, he stopped at the desk on the way out and was presented with the bill. He had a heart attack on the spot and died. Some family members surmise that the bill may have been more than expected.

His brother Frank, also known as Peppers, had died of a heart attack three years earlier, but his death was more comprehensible. Uncle Peppers owned a candy store next to Wilson Avenue Elementary School. It was not only frequented by grade school kids who bought shakes and penny candy but was also a hangout for the neighborhood guys and their friends. I never quite understood the connection, but Uncle Peppers was a bookie for those who played the numbers—housewives, school teachers, truck drivers and others. Among the regulars at the store were several cops, including a state trooper, a local patrolman, and a city detective. They knew what was going on but looked the other way and sometimes checked the paper to see if they had hit the number.

It was a colorful crowd of characters that hung out there—Stash, Pee Wee, Curly, Moonman, Plywood, Eggy, Porky. (There were other acquaintances of the family with such pseudonyms as Slug, Cigar-face, Ray Rats, and Louis the Lug. I never knew the real names of most of them.) The stories that they told could have made a movie script or filled a police blotter—and definitely the dime novels with their copious sexcapades.

When I was in grade school at Wilson Avenue, I would stop in each day, and Peppers would offer me a soda or shake or a burger. He had a room in the back with a bed, and I would sometimes sack out there, particularly in later years when I came home from college.

The luncheonette was one of the places where I might encounter my father. Dad always seemed to have a routine, like the early insurance agents making their rounds. He would stop at Peppers's store, his own "Office Bar and Grill" across the street, or any number of social clubs in the Ironbound where a card game might be going on.

Watching Uncle Peppers grill a hamburger was a lesson in concocting a delicious, slow-acting poison. The liquid fat released from the ground beef was reintroduced into the burning meat or scraped to the side of the grill to be intermingled with the fried potatoes and peppers which were heaped on a bun with the burger. Eating his own food may have caused his fatal heart attack.

Peppers got sick on a trip to Italy. He came home and was hospitalized with a heart attack. The day he was discharged he went bowling so as not to disappoint his teammates. It was then that he suffered his fatal heart attack. His arteries must have been sealed shut from all the grease he ate.

Gray Matter, Dark Matter, and Doesn't Matter

Uncle Peppers, like most of the Serios, was generous, fun-loving, and most likely felt that regardless of what he did, what he ate, and the late hours he kept, he would live forever. Like Gene, he never married, and they were the first of Luigi's children to leave this life.

It is not the brevity of life that is important but its meaning and relevance. Future generations may not remember Peppers, but he served as a catalyst for other events, some of which will also be forgotten. In his short time at his candy store, he provided a place of meeting where other connections were made, actions stimulated, and friendships affirmed. Peppers added his own color to the human mix. There are people in life who serve no other purpose than to be there. And that seems to be enough.

When I remember Uncle Peppers I am reminded of Raphael Sabatini's description of Scaramouche: "He was born with the gift of laughter and a sense that the world was mad."[1] We may not be able to choose our parents or the environment into which we are born or the influences imposed upon us, but we can determine our future as we face the madness of this world with a sense of humor.

1. Sabatini, *Scaramouche*, 3

CATTITUDES

I watch my cat stare into empty space. Has she seen a mouse that I cannot see? Is she waiting for something to happen? Is she pondering some deep mystery of cat philosophy? Is she simply practicing the art of mindfulness and her own expression of Transcendental Meditation? Aside from using the brain for the normal means of functioning in the world, what really occurs within the mind of a cat?

In the many years that cats have resided with us, all have manifested their unique personalities in an assortment of expressions. All have displayed varying degrees of affection and disdain, as well as behavior that mystifies the ordinary observer. I name my cats since I don't know what they call themselves. Over the course of their lifetimes, I have noticed that they have become what I have named them.

Topcat was very small and would squeeze her body into a cabinet to sleep in a bread pan. When Mary Ann was ready to bake, she would first have to empty the slumbering feline who was usually guarded by her protective canine, Underdog, a friendly beagle and loving companion.

Pyewacket drowned mice in the toilet. Not only live mice that he would catch but the fabricated church mice that Mary Ann would make for the church bazaar. When he could not find any mice, he purloined the kids' rolled-up socks and dropped them in the toilet. Pyewacket was very fastidious and usually washed his food before consuming it.

Locutus, whom we called "Q," was a food poacher. He would sit next to me at the kitchen table, and as I raised my fork, he would extend his paw in an effort to divert the morsel from my mouth to his. He was named after the *Star Trek* character who challenges reality but even more so for the German *quelle*, which means "hidden."

Othello, named after Shakespeare's Moor of Venice, was a large quiet cat that my daughter, Tasha, had rescued from a bear trap when she found him struggling along the side of the road. The vet had to amputate part of his paw, but we believe he appreciated the aid that we gave him. He was very shy and would seek a hiding place when other family and guests would come to visit. There was one time that he attempted to be friendly by jumping up into the lap of my visiting aunt, startling her enough to let out a loud scream. Both cat and aunt seemed to be equally terrified, and Othello went back to his hiding place. He displayed an almost human quality of caring when Pyewacket took ill and subsequently died. I have noticed that in other cats as well who went into hospice mode when their companions were preparing to pass on. Othello lived to the extraordinary age of twenty-eight.

Sakhmet was named after the Egyptian lioness goddess and personified all the negative female characteristics. She was very jealous and would steal jewelry and anything that glittered, especially gold, and conceal it in her hidden lair. A rather selfish cat, self-centered, she would cry if she didn't get her way.

Zeus, who may have possessed some Maine Coon ancestry, didn't like anything new. If he could vote, he would be a right-wing conservative. I would not like to argue politics with him, even though he was polite and good-natured. His sister, Maggie, was his food taster, since he apparently had a fear of being poisoned. He also was afraid of being alone and was very dependent upon his human staff.

Magnificat, whom we called Maggie, was the personification of the curious cat. She always wanted to check things out but not be involved with anyone. Maggie was anti-social, except at mealtimes when she would sit on the kitchen table, waiting for handouts. She did not like to be covered with a blanket or picked up, and she snored very loudly.

Cats, like any other species, operate within their own worlds. However, when you consider the behavior of all of our cats, their actions are consistent with Darwin's evolutionary thesis, namely the instinct for survival and self-preservation and the preservation of its species. Cats are both predators and prey. They are constantly looking for food, and they seek out anything that gives them satisfaction or ensures their continued well-being. They have a fear of anything that is perceived as a threat, whether it is an unfamiliar visitor or a sudden movement. Cats may also exhibit friendship, even affection, associating with anyone that may offer protection.

There have been moments when I have seen my cat just staring into space. If he was at the window, I could understand his observation of the passing scene, some activity or person, or another animal, but when he is just pondering nothingness, it raises some questions about what cats are actually thinking. In his mindfulness sessions, is he aware of himself and his place in this world?

Can I expect my cat to think and behave rationally when reason seems to be a limited human function? Humans set standards of behavior to which there are mental reservations that may be beyond our comprehension. There are those who confine themselves to the empirical world, that which their senses and their reason create within their minds. There are some who believe in a world beyond our perception. However, the fact that we can conceive of a world beyond the normal brings it into the realm of possibility.

The behavior of cats should be considered in the context of any species' need for survival, whether their behavior appears to be antagonistic, aggressive, threatening, terroristic or loving, affectionate, tolerant, or ambivalent. Even then, we must question whether we are attributing meaning to a cat's personality based on our own observations and our own interpretations of their behavior. They catalyze our own perspective on life.

THE VOICE OF
MANY ANGELS

The Kutztown Area Historical Society dedicated a room in the 1892 Public School Building where a beloved teacher, Mildred Corrigan, had taught sixth grade. Mildred was a member of my church, and I was asked to give the dedicatory prayer. During the afternoon many stories were told, not only about Mildred, but about beloved teachers who taught more by how they lived than by what they said. More than history or math or grammar, they were life lessons that shaped our behavior forever. Not all teachers were able to change lives in positive ways, and not all students were able to be transformed constructively, but the potential to change the world was always there. Words are seeds, and we never know into what soil they will be sown or how they will germinate and be nourished.

Our lives can be transformed in a moment, in a chance encounter, in the twinkling of an eye. But a lifetime can go into the preparation for that moment.

In the film *Finding Forrester*, William Forrester is a reclusive Pulitzer Prize-winning author who never published a second book. He spends several decades sequestered in his top-floor Bronx apartment monitoring the changes in the world through his window and his three television sets. Forrester, played by Sean Connery, is godlike. At least some would imagine God that way— all-wise and all-knowing, remote from the world, observing it but not interacting with it. A God who performed some miracles a few thousand years ago, but what has he done since?

But then an exceptionally gifted but underachieving Black sixteen-year-old breaks into his apartment, and the latent chemistry begins to work through their interaction, catalyzing both their lives. What hasn't happened in a lifetime happens overnight. We can live an entire lifetime for one transforming moment that redeems our entire existence and gives meaning to our walk in the sun. To live for that moment of metamorphosis when we are changed and when we can change the life of another person for the better justifies our existence.

After my brother died I came across some audio tapes that Bob had recorded. They were his thoughts for a sermon he had intended to preach. Bob had studied for the priesthood and had graduated from seminary but decided not to take holy orders. He became a high school principal instead. His thoughts on one of those tapes were about angels, about people who had come into his life at various times, spoken a word of encouragement or did a kind deed unexpectedly, or were simply there in a moment of despair and loneliness. They were his angels, and he began to see more and more of their presence as his life ebbed away.

We all have our angel stories to tell: the mysterious stranger who shows up in a time of crisis to comfort and help and then is gone, the sudden and inexplicable healing, the gift that offers hope in a time of despair, the bringers of rainbows when we seem abandoned and forsaken.

We are angels to each other, emissaries of God whose words of encouragement and hope, whose acts of love and whose presence in times of need represent the presence of Christ. We may not realize the influence we have on each other, and we may live an entire life for that redeeming moment when one little word, one little deed will change the world. This is why we need to value community; we do not exist in isolation but in symbiosis. I once gave a lecture about the Gaia Principle, how the earth was a living organism affected by the interaction of all life forms. But the universe is also a living soul, infused with the Spirit of God that is in all things. The divine that is in you resonates with the divine that is in me, and collectively, whether organized through religion or the church or some other agency, can become the manifestation of God's presence in the world. The universe is a sacred community, as Teilhard de Chardin describes it, and in the sacred community love changes those who love as well as those who are loved.

The prophet John, in his celestial vision of the last days, wrote:

> Then I looked, and I heard the voice of many angels surrounding the throne and the living creatures and the elders; they numbered myriads of myriads and thousands of thousands, singing with full voice,
>
> "Worthy is the Lamb that was slaughtered to receive power and wealth and wisdom and might and honor and glory and blessing!" Then I heard every creature in heaven and on earth and under the earth and in the sea, and all that is in them, singing, "To the one seated on the throne and to the Lamb be blessing and honor and glory and might forever and ever!"
>
> (Rev 5:11–13)

A hallelujah chorus of all creation praising God.

The voice of many angels is the collective goodness of all people, in many ways and at many times making a positive impact upon the world so that at the end of time the Christ Spirit is universally acclaimed and all creation acknowledges that love is indeed supreme.

Go out and change the world by caring for it and for other humans. Let your acts of love honor your creator and the reason for your being. Let your voice be one of many angels.

THE GOLDEN LAMP

A mong the Sufis, the mystical branch of Islam, there are the delightful stories of Nasrudin. One day, a friend found Nasrudin in his front yard looking for the key to his house. After helping him search for a while, the friend asked Nasrudin where he thought he might have dropped the key. Nasrudin said he dropped it on the floor inside the house. "Then why are you looking outside for it?" "Because," said Nasrudin, "there is more light here."

Light is necessary for seeing. Perhaps that's why light is the first thing God created, according to Genesis. (God could see what God was doing?) In Saint John's vision of the celestial city, there is "no need of sun or moon to shine on it, for the glory of God is its light" (Rev 21:23). Christ is the lamp, the light by which men and women will perceive one another.

I have always thought it interesting that we never really see one another. What we see is only reflected light. Remove a light source from an object and it becomes invisible. In this world, we depend upon an outside source in order to perceive anything. We must hold up a lamp in order to see and understand and interpret our lives. It is no wonder, therefore, that ever since Diogenes took a lamp in search of truth, in his quest for an honest man, the oil lamp has been the symbol of education and learning. God creates light first because God knows that knowledge is essential to life and growth.

Our spiritual forebears recognized this. One of my predecessors at St. John's United Church of Christ, Rev. J. Sassaman

Herman, was a leader in lighting the lamp of education in our community. He felt that one must use knowledge and reason to discern the truth that lies behind the words of Holy Scripture. In 1860, in consultation with the struggling Reformed college, Franklin and Marshall in Lancaster, Pennsylvania, he opened his parsonage to five students, who were taught by Henry R. Nicks. Nicks had studied at the Mercersburg Theological Seminary which later became Lancaster Theological Seminary, my alma mater.

This school in the St. John's parsonage was called Fairview Seminary. Among its first five students was Nathan C. Schaffer who later became principal of the Keystone State Normal School, which eventually morphed into the present day Kutztown University.

The spiritual ancestors of the United Church of Christ were likewise responsible for the first institutions of higher education in this country. The UCC denomination was the result of a 1957 merger of the Congregational Christian Churches who were primarily located in New England and descended from the early pilgrims; and the Evangelical and Reformed Church, concentrated in the Missouri River Valley and in Pennsylvania. All four of these constituent groups—Congregational, Christian, Evangelical, Reformed—derived their theology and practice from the great reformers—Martin Luther, Ulrich Zwingli, and John Calvin—and emigrated to this country from England and Germany.

One of the cardinal principals of Luther's theology was justification by grace through faith. Our salvation comes by our faith, and our faith is predicated upon our understanding of the Scripture, which each individual Christian is responsible for knowing. In order to read and understand the Scripture, learning was critical, not only in the training of pastors but for the person in the pew. (Some church members often complained that they needed a university degree in order to understand the erudite and complex sermons of some pastors. Thus, the observation that some pastors were six days invisible and on the seventh day, incomprehensible).

It was my early predecessors of the United Church of Christ that founded Harvard and Yale Universities. Harvard was named after John Harvard, a Puritan minister described as "a godly gentleman and a lover of learning," Its purpose was to train pastors for the churches of the new colony. Its divinity schools are still related by history and tradition to the United Church of Christ. Gallaudet, the first college for the deaf, was also founded by a Congregationalist minister, Thomas Gallaudet. The first college for women, Oberlin, and many others trace their origins to the UCC. Today, thirty colleges and thirteen seminaries, including Chicago, Vanderbilt, and Union are related to this denomination.

We honor our forebears who carried the golden lamp of learning to illumine a path of opportunity through a world of poverty, ignorance, and social and racial prejudice. When the Civil War ended and the slaves were freed, it was the American Missionary Association of our church that established Black colleges throughout the South. Today this denomination has just as strong a commitment to higher education, and we continue to honor our heritage by keeping the golden lamp burning where we are.

In both testaments of holy scripture, light is significant to spiritual imagery. "The Lord is my light," the psalmist says (Ps 27:1). This light is a symbol of goodness, uprightness, and blessing. Again and again, this light is used to describe the way of God in the world and the mission of Jesus. The Gospels present Jesus as the light bearer. "In him was life, and the life was the light of men" (John 1:4). Those who have the light of Christ within them illumine the lives of others.

Our history books are filled with the stories of men and women who were born into lives of poverty and degradation and were forced to live in the darkness of despair. And yet, because of an inner light, a dimly burning lamp with their souls, they were able to surmount their obstacles and become a light to others.

There's a parable in each of these individuals. Darkness is not always something that is thrust upon us, for which we have no responsibility. Darkness can also symbolize ignorance and a set of values without reference to God—the values of materialism, of concern only for self, and the satisfaction of immediate pleasures without regard to the needs of others. Darkness also symbolizes lostness—life without direction or principles to give it depth and meaning.

Light represents values opposite to that of darkness—priority of love, concern for the spiritual dimensions of life, and a person whose life principles give substance and meaning to life.

Perhaps Nasrudin was right. We should not only walk in the light but bring the light to where it is needed, where we can find the key to life and its meaning.

This is the light of Christ, the lamp of God. The kind of light that leads to the city whose light source is the glory of God. In the kingdom of heaven, the source of light is God himself, the totality of wisdom. Let us live in the kingdom of God now by bearing our light in this world.

CHURCH BUILDING
ABANDONED

It was a small, wooden building on the edge of the university campus, built sometime during the 1930s, perhaps a WPA project. Some faculty, mostly theater department people, and a few students had used it as a church. There wasn't much to it—one large room and a big closet near the door that served as a pastor's study. There really wasn't a pastor, only someone who enlisted others to prepare an agenda for their weekly gatherings. One of the music faculty had donated a parlor pump organ that she no longer had need of.

And now, almost a century later, a group of people were meeting to discuss the building's demolition or sale. The head of the theater department presided.

As members of the committee were entering the building on a rainy Wednesday evening and talking with one another, an older woman came in. She was not a member of the committee but mistakenly believed that it was a church gathering, perhaps a mid-week prayer meeting. However, she very much needed a place to pray. Her only daughter, her son-in-law, and their baby had died in the recent flood. She was all alone.

The woman tearfully told her story to the group, not realizing that it wasn't a church gathering. And then she saw the old organ and asked if she could play a hymn that had always given her comfort in times of distress. To everyone's knowledge, it had never been played and it wasn't known if it still worked. But it did. And the woman played "Nearer My God to Thee."

Across the room, the professor was holding back tears and trembling. When the woman finished playing, she was surrounded by the group and embraced. The love and comfort were abundant as each person offered whatever help and consolation they could.

The woman thanked them and then walked out into the rain and disappeared into the darkness but now bearing the light of newfound caring friends.

The committee of twelve convened, and all were in agreement that they could not demolish the building. That small group had become a church and they agreed to continue to meet to share one another's pain, and help each other—and others—bear the pain of the world and their own personal troubles. They would not call themselves a "church" since there were two Muslims and a Jew among them. Nevertheless, they were a people who came together to encounter the deeper spiritual meaning of their lives and acknowledge that they were more than they appeared to be. They pledged to communicate with each other and to share their journeys through life, to learn from one another, and to support each other through all the crises of living.

Even if they had agreed to take down the building and never meet again, for that one brief hour, they were what Christians call the church, the embodiment of the love of God poured out in their concern for a woman in need of love in her time of despair. That truly is the meaning of the Christ, the avatar of God, the incarnation of the Spirit of God, a love that we could see and experience.

We are all called to be the Christ to each other. Buddhists would say that the spirit of God in me recognizes the spirit of God in you, and therefore we are all of one spirit and need to love and support each other.

TO KNOW THE PLACE
WHERE YOU BELONG

We learn much during our high school years, some of which would prove useful in later years. And there is much that we would never use again.

Nick was a classmate and a very good friend. His parents owned and operated a luncheonette and soda fountain on Pacific Street in Newark, a good place to hang out and observe the passing scene, as well as to acquire some skills that one might find useful in dealing with the opposite sex.

A dance in the East Side High gym was coming up and all I knew was the old-fashioned two-step. It was good enough to hold a girl close, but I wanted to broaden my dancing repertoire. Nick's sister offered to teach me the cha-cha, so in the back room of the luncheonette, Marie taught me the right moves.

It turned out that the Halloween Dance was a costume event, so I rented the uniform of a Revolutionary War officer. It felt kind of silly walking the streets dressed as George Washington, but Washington doing the cha-cha was even more ridiculous. I suppose that with all those saxes in the band, I shouldn't have expected minuets. The dance ended with the unofficial school song, Earle Hagen's jazzy "Harlem Nocturne." It was another teen experience to remember.

Nick raised pigeons as a hobby. On his roof, there was a cage full of the birds which he would let loose on occasion so that they could stretch their wings. Sometimes a few would take off and find other nesting places, so every once in a while he would go to Hoboken to buy more pigeons. It reminded me of the scenes in the movie *On the Waterfront* where Terry Malloy has pigeons on the roof, and of course the movie was filmed in Hoboken.

Hoboken was a short ride over the Passaic and Hackensack Rivers from Newark, using the then-engineering marvel of the world, the Pulaski Skyway. I drove Nick to get his pigeons one time, but I wanted to take a brief detour to see where Frank Sinatra had lived as a child. He had lived at 415 Monroe Street in Hoboken, and I had lived at 145 Monroe Street in Newark. I thought there was something auspicious in that. My mother apparently knew Frank. She had a picture with him, now lost, and his autograph. Frank's home burned down a couple of years later.

That summer I was planning to drive out to Orwigsburg, Pennsylvania, to visit a friend that I had met at camp. Nick asked if I would take a few crates of pigeons to see if they could find their way back from over a hundred miles away. He speculated that some of his pigeons might find mates in Pennsylvania and decide to stay there. I asked him if it wasn't illegal to transport pigeons over the state line for immoral purposes.

We packed the three crates of pigeons in the trunk of my Oldsmobile and I took off on the three-hour drive. (This was before the interstate highways.) In my friend Bruce's backyard, we released the birds. Of the more than sixty pigeons, all but four returned to their home in Newark, but why didn't they return to Hoboken? In the past, carrier pigeons were used by the post office to deliver mail. They were extensively used during World War II to deliver battleground messages. The Taliban even banned the owning of pigeons to prevent reports of their actions from escaping Afghanistan.

What is there in the instinct of pigeons that compels them to return to the place of their origin, sometimes flying over a thousand miles? What is there in our own minds that drives us back to the places we knew when we were younger, back in memory, back in the desire to return?

Pigeons are not the only animals that can navigate back to their origins. From the migrations of monarch butterflies to the dogs that made transcontinental journeys to the homes of those who loved and cared for them, many species have some sort of GPS system built in them that enables them to know the place where they belong.

Some scientists have suggested that birds observe the landmarks on their flight and are thus able to remember them so that they can return. But the pigeons I transported were locked in a darkened car trunk. They could not remember landmarks. Other scientists have speculated that some animals, like sea turtles and salmon, have inherent magnetic sensors that aid in the alignment with the earth's magnetic field, giving a new twist on the term "animal magnetism."

Humans also have an innate desire to return to their origin, to be at one with their creator, whether it is a mythical Eden or heaven or cosmic consciousness. It is a place to feel safe, a place to feel like one belongs, a place to feel like home. The old spiritual "Steal Away" may have referred to escaping the pain and suffering of slavery, but it also has an eternal message of being called home:

> My Lord, He calls me,
> He calls me by the thunder;
> The trumpet sounds within my soul;
> I ain't got long to stay here.

We have heard the phrase "life is a journey, not a destination" so often that we tend to miss its meaning. Our desire is to return to God which we consider the ultimate destination. However, God is always with us on our journey, so that the journey becomes the destination, and the awareness of the presence of God within us and around us is where we belong. T. S. Eliot may have intended something else, but he was right when he said, "We shall not cease from exploration, and the end of all our exploring will be to arrive where we started and know the place for the first time."[1]

---

1. Eliot, "We Shall Not Cease . . ."

Gray Matter, Dark Matter, and Doesn't Matter

I have opened a box of Christmas cards received from family and friends more than fifty years ago. Most have passed on and the messages about their lives seem no longer relevant, but the memories are there. And so are the memories from high school, learning to dance, transporting pigeons, and a million other encounters with life and fellow travelers. They have all shaped who I have become and who I will be, and I am at home in the heart of God. As are we all.

BIBLIOGRAPHY

Bates, Katherine Lee. "O Beautiful Spacious Skies." *The Hymnal*. St. Louis: Eden, 1941.

Berendt, Joachim-Ernst. *The World Is Sound: Nada Brahma: Music and the Landscape of Consciousness*. Rochester, VT: Destiny, 1983.

Bustard, Ned, ed. *It Was Good: Making Art to the Glory of God*. Baltimore: Square Halo, 2006.

Campbell, Don. *The Mozart Effect*. New York: Avon, 1997.

Casti, John L. *Paradigms Lost*. New York: Avon, 1989.

Cox, Harvey. *On Not Leaving It to the Snake*. Toronto: Macmillan. 1964.

Crick, Francis. *Life Itself: Its Origin and Nature*. New York: Simon and Schuster. 1981.

Dao, Christine. "Man of Science, Man of God: Johann Kepler." Institute for Creation and Research, Mar 1, 2008. https://www.icr.org/article/science-man-god-johann-kepler.

Dawkins, Richard. *The God Delusion*. New York: Houghton Mifflin, 2006.

Eliot, T. S. "We Shall Not Cease . . ." https://www.goodreads.com/quotes /644987-we-shall-not-cease-from-exploration-and-the-end-of.

Ensley, Eddie. *Visions: The Soul's Path to the Sacred*. Chicago: Loyola. 2000.

Franklin, Benjamin. "For Want of a Nail . . ." https://www.goodreads.com/ quotes/tag/poor-richard-s-almanac

Freud, Sigmund. *The Future of an Illusion*. W. W. Norton, 1989.

Friedmann, Jonathan L. "*Kippot* in Jewish Custom." https://www.jewishmag. com/122mag/kippa%5Ckippa.htm.

Gowan, John Curtis. *Trance, Art and Creativity*. Northridge, CA: Privately Printed, 1975

Jaynes, Julian. *The Origins of Consciousness in the Breakdown of the Bicameral Mind*. New York: Houghton Mifflin, 1973.

Kalidasa. "Look to This Day." https://allpoetry.com/Look-To-This-Day.

Kelsey, Morton T. *God, Dreams, and Revelation*. Minneapolis: Augsburg, 1974.

Lowell, James Russell. "The Present Crisis." https://allpoetry.com/The-Present-Crisis.

MacLeod, *Only One Way Left*. Glasgow: Iona Community, 1956.

"Majorities of U.S. Adults Say They Believe in Heaven, Hell." Pew Research Center. https://www.pewresearch.org/religion/2021/11/23/views-on-the-afterlife/.

Millay, Edna St. Vincent. "Ashes of Life." https://www.poetryfoundation.org/poems/44717/ashes-of-life.

Newell, J. Philip. *Listening for the Heartbeat of God*. New York: Paulist, 1997.

Pope, Alexander. "An Essay on Criticism." Part 2. https://www.poetryfoundation.org/articles/69379/an-essay-on-criticism.

Rohr, Richard, and Friends. *Contemplation in Action*. New York: Crossroad, 2006.

Sabatini, Rafael. *Scaramouche: A Romance of the French Revolution*. New York: W. W. Norton, 2002.

Sagan, Carl, and Druyan, Ann. *Shadows of Forgotten Ancestors*. New York: Random House, 1992

Sanford, John A. *Dreams: God's Forgotten Language*. New York: J. B. Lippincott, 1968.

Serio, Harry L. *The Mysticism of Ordinary and Extraordinary Experience*. Eugene, OR: Wipf and Stock, 2021.

Shakespeare, William. *The Globe Illustrated Shakespeare*. Edited by Howard Staunton. New York: Greenwich House, 1983.

Spong, John Shelby. *Why Christianity Must Change or Die*. New York: HarperCollins, 1998.

Thoreau, Henry David. "If a Man Does Not Keep Pace . . ." https://www.goodreads.com/quotes/438500-if-a-man-does-not-keep-pace-with-his-companions.

Tucker, Jim B. *Life before Life: A Scientific Investigation of Children's Memories of Previous Lives*. New York: St. Martin's, 2005.

Tyson, Neil DeGrasse. "The Atoms of Our Bodies . . ." Goodreads. https://www.goodreads.com/quotes/484586-the-atoms-of-our-bodies-are-traceable-to-stars-that.

Watterson, Bill. "The Surest Sign. . ." https://www.brainyquote.com/quotes/bill_watterson_105988.

Printed in the USA
CPSIA information can be obtained
at www.ICGtesting.com
LVHW010317120724
785254LV00002B/178

9 798385 223459